TREASURES
OF THE
LOST RACES

By
Rene Noorbergen

TEACH Services, Inc.
Brushton, New York

2007 08 09 10 11 12 · 5 4 3 2 1

Copyright © 2004 TEACH Services, Inc. and Judie D. Noorbergen
ISBN-13: 978-1-57258-267-5
ISBN-10: 1-57258-267-7
Library of Congress Control Number: 2004102055

Published by

TEACH Services, Inc.
www.TEACHServices.com

To the treasure that has been found, yet not displayed;
discovered, yet still waiting to be revealed
August 27/28, 1981

TABLE OF CONTENTS

FOREWORD

This is a book about treasure—have no doubt about that. In fact, it may even help you find some on your own! But it is primarily a book about the games Mother Earth has played with the treasures reluctantly entrusted to her throughout her thousands of years of existence. Needless to say, the researching and writing of *Treasures of the Lost Races* gave rise to special moments of agony and ecstasy; the inordinate pains and pleasures that are experienced when man is in touch with nature.

The earth has taken in the relics of past civilizations like a sponge, absorbing all and relinquishing little, even when pressured. In going through the annals and reports of archaeological history, in trying to wring the earth's secrets from her, I sometimes began to feel like a little boy, waiting with barely concealed excitement for what would eventually issue forth . . .

Little individual pieces don't mean all that much when extracted from the earth and examined separately; only when combined or placed within the right context does a strange and sometimes unfamiliar pattern emerge, slowly bringing to light new discoveries about the nations of old. As is true of all of us, I knew little bits about many big things; but not until the target was defined did I initiate a concentrated effort to search for the specific things that I felt would be representative of what the earth has been hiding from us all these many centuries.

Combing through the dry, unimaginative reports written by no-nonsense scientists and visiting those places where the spades of the "romantic science"—archaeology—have brought dead and forgotten societies back to life has put some sites of ancient civilizations into a new perspective. In fact, some of the more recent discoveries have practically "repainted" the map of the ancient world, and are beginning to reintroduce us to people who might otherwise have been forgotten. Not only were these people in some cases technologically superior to us, but many of them had the rare ability to find form for their intimate feelings about men and nature, producing artwork of unequaled beauty.

And now the search for their treasures is on.

Reports on the gold artifacts that have been retrieved from ancient tombs, along with stories about the caches of valuable coins that have been found in the most unexpected places, have sparked the imagination—and the greed—of a brand-new breed of gold diggers. This in turn has created a totally new market for the twentieth-century metal-detecting business. Millions of dollars are now being spent annually by archaeological adventurers, all with the hope that their discoveries will eventually justify their investment.

The skyrocketing price of gold in the early 1980s has been one of the contributing causes of this mad search for precious metals. Any time that gold—the ultimate standard of wealth—rises in value, people are bound to speculate. The upward move from $34.85 per ounce in 1970 to $850.00 in 1980 brought even more adventurers into the market. Investing in gold *stock* is a passive activity; to put even a relatively small amount into prospecting and metal-detection equipment, on the other hand, calls for active involvement and can provide fun for the entire family. And when the investor in turn hits "pay dirt" (literally speaking!), the rewards can be enormous.

Gold has held a strange fascination for men ever since our early ancestors were attracted to its unique qualities. It cannot corrode, does not tarnish, is not affected by the passing of time, and will not lose density or any of its other physical properties when melted down.

We cannot even guess at the number or the size of the gold objects presumed to be still hidden under the surface of the earth, but the largest one ever recovered was the solid-gold coffin of King Tut-ankh-amon, which weighs 2,447 pounds. The largest gold nugget ever found was discovered in Victoria, Australia, by prospectors John Deason and Richard Oates in 1860. It weighed 150 pounds and measured 21 inches long and 10 inches across. Judged to be almost one hundred percent pure, it was sold for close to $50,000.

The big problem with finding gold is that huge nuggets or voluminous quantities in any form are rare. Yet some gold can be found, provided one wants it badly enough. Sea water, for example, is known to contain ten milligrams of gold for every ton of water; this means that no less that 2,835 tons of sea water would have to be filtered and purified to obtain one single ounce of gold. Dr. Fritz Haber, a German scientist concerned about how his country would pay her World War I debts, came upon the novel idea of filtering the gold from the water of the North Sea, but his plan failed miserably. Modern science has advanced so that it is now entirely possible to change other metals such as lead or platinum into gold by means of nuclear fission. The only problem is that the gold thus produced would cost more than its market value.

Nevertheless, since man's hunger for gold is insatiable, it may eventually become necessary to find a practical way to filter the sea. In the meantime, occasional discoveries of new land deposits keep today's prospectors' dreams alive. The Brazilian gold rush which started in the 1980s is still attracting explorers by the hundreds to the steaming jungle, where in Serra Pelada, sixty miles from Maraba, millionaires are made daily. One prospector, Jose Maria da Silva, thirty-five, arrived there hungry in April of 1980 and was obliged to borrow money for food. Within fifteen days he was able to repay the loan out of the twenty-two pounds of gold he had discovered. Now, because of his steadily growing fortune, he is known as King of Serra Pelada. One plot he prospected netted him twelve million dollars in gold within three short months! On one day alone da Silva extracted seven hundred pounds of gold from the hot, steaming soil, earning for his day's work $4.75 million . . .

On the other side of the world, in Australia, a four-man prospecting expedition recently claimed to have found the legendary El Dorado of Australian folklore, Lasseter's Lost Reef, a vein of gold believed to be twelve miles long. It was first discovered in 1897 by Harold Lasseter, the son of an English miner. But even though he had finally by 1930 raised sufficient funds to return to the site and continue his work, hardships were so numerous that the expedition broke up, and Lasseter took two of the camels and went ahead alone. His body was found two years later by trackers combing the area. He had never revealed to anyone the exact location of his find.

The new discoverer of the reef, Nick Delaraine, claims that he came across a mound of gold quartz three or four feet below the ground. He asserted that it went on for miles, but that his party were unable to take samples because of shotgun-armed natives and a white ranger who forced them off the territory. His attempts to secure a mining permit from the government for the area specified have failed thus far; there are those who claim that the Australian government has ulterior motives for the delaying tactics and really has no intention of issuing a permit at all.

But aside from the occasional gold strike and discoveries such as these, man's quest for gold has been limited to searching for buried treasure; changing base metals into gold—the alchemists' dream; or extracting gold from the oceans. But space-age technology is beginning to change those dreams, for with the introduction of rocketry, the siren song of gold is now drawing treasure hunters toward other planets; and, given man's preoccupation with the acquisition of wealth, chances that he will succeed in reaching the mineral deposits in outer space are good— *very* good.

The idea of gathering gold from the vastness of space is in itself nothing new. In the seventeenth century, alchemists had already discovered that the meteorites that bombarded the earth contained small quantities of precious metal; in fact, the value of meteorites in those years was determined not by their origin but rather by their content of such metals. Based on sample analysis, it has been estimated that a single iron asteroid 100 meters (328 feet) in diameter may contain as much as one billion dollars' worth of platinum, gold, osmium and other precious metals. Careful calculations performed by leading astronomers today indicate that there are about 200,000 of these asteroids orbiting the sun.

Listening to astronomers and engineers discuss the possibility of sending mining expeditions into space is like being back in the frontier days, when it was necessary to weigh the danger of venturing into unknown territory against the treasures waiting to be discovered. The most promising types of asteroids appear to be the Apollo and Amor variety, Apollos being those bodies whose orbits cross the earth's path, and Amors those asteroids that are much more elliptical and approach but do not cross the earth's orbit.

No one knows as yet how may of these Apollos and Amors are in our immediate vicinity, but the number of discovered asteroids is climbing year by year, thanks to Dr. Eleanor Helin of Mt. Palomar Observatory. Dr. Helin, with her eighteen-inch Schmidt wide-angle camera, continually photographs the starlit skies, turning up three or four new asteroids per year. Only forty-seven have been found to date, but conservative estimates place the total number passing close to the earth at somewhere between 800 and 2,400, while the total number of 100-meter objects suitable for mining is thought to be in the vicinity of 100,000. Granted, there are lots of "ifs" to this subject, but by the time the first asteroid expedition is ready to be launched, more targets will have been discovered and isolated. Even one asteroid cannot be depleted in one expedition, so with forty-seven already mapped and ready for exploration, the search for more asteroids is not an A-1 priority.

A number of interested private groups have already laid much of the groundwork for asteroid mining. It has been reported that a contingent of NASA engineers involved in an organization known as the World Space Foundation have already given a $10,000 grant to Dr. Helin to fund her search for additional asteroids. Even the method of extracting their precious metals has already been worked out. Dr. Jack Arnold of the University of California has found that crushing chondrite meteorite stone between steel rollers pulverizes the highly magnetic iron fragments and allows them to be separated from the silicate debris. Gold and platinum should also come out during the process, since they have a chemical affinity for iron.

There is little doubt that space mining will be a highly profitable venture. Let's assume that the retrievable pre-

cious metals in the average 100-meter asteroid are worth a
billion dollars. Subtract from this a few hundred million
for the hardware and for the expedition's expenses, and
the investment in both time and money would still seem to
be well worth while.

In the meantime, we're earthbound; and the search for
gold in space has really very little to do with the search for
ancient treasure on this globe, even though some highly
imaginative writers have already suggested that many of
the discovered treasures are in all probability "gifts from
the gods from outer space" to their earthbound cousins.

But in searching for the treasure of the ancients, we
have to deal with reality, along with the legends, traditions and an occasional hunch. Combine these with the
newest tools available to archaeology, and we have a
promising future indeed.

Finding treasure in whatever form and from whatever
tribe or race, and then attempting to track down its origin, brings with it an incomparable sense of excitement
and exhilaration. It is a search for adventure that will
never end.

In this world of limitations, that in itself is a major discovery.

Rene Noorbergen
Collegedale, Tennessee
April 1982

CHAPTER 1

Archaeology—the Romantic Science

When historians define their subject as a "chronological record of events," they are *leaning* toward the truth—but only leaning. For whereas this definition may aptly apply to a person's medical background, family tree or some other chain of continuing events that can be easily traced, historians have barely scratched the surface of the true history of the earth.

And what a surface it is!

Scarred by cataclysmic earthquakes, volcanic eruptions and devastating floods, and bombarded by an uncountable number of meteorites of varying sizes for thousands of years, the thin, rocky crust that covers our planet's molten core has undergone so many transformations that its current pockmarked face bears no resemblance to its original facade. The earth has been tortured unmercifully by the savage hands of time and bears the scars to prove it.

It has often been said that our imagination is the only quality that separates us as humans from the rest of the animal kingdom. Yet what really transpired on this planet during the early years of its development reaches far beyond our comprehension. Since the beginning of the twentieth century, science has made gigantic strides forward into outer space. But when it comes to relating the intricate details of our own distant history we stand mute. The *ooparts*—out-of-place artifacts—that have been uncovered over the years (see *Secrets of the Lost Races*) have introduced serious doubts into our concept of history. While they have enabled us to retrieve from antiquity minute details which have increased our understanding of the ancients, they have also intensified our bewilderment and stimulated our desire to learn more and more about those who have gone before us.

Our globe has had a catastrophic history—of that there is no doubt—and its human occupants are responsible for much of it. Apparently not satisfied with the intensity of natural calamities that disturbed the serenity of the blue planet, tribal warfare, rampaging armies, conquering despots and merciless tyrants have engulfed entire continents in practically continuous warfare, sometimes uprooting entire civilizations and destroying everything in their paths.

When looking at the ooparts of the past, it really doesn't take much imagination to realize that the silent unknown has hidden from us the stories of people whose lives might have been open books if their legacy had not been crushed by avenging armies. The ruthlessness of the Islamic conquerors and the brutal devastation and savage slaughter of humanity wrought by the Roman armies are but token examples of the upheavals caused by the unpredictability of the earth's confused occupants. And whenever plundering armies approached or civil unrest threatened, frightened people gathered their belongings and fled into the hills and onto the beaches in order to hide their treasures in remote places considered unlikely to attract the greedy eyes of the frenzied looters. Sometimes they hid them so well that the treasure troves remained entombed for thousands of years, awaiting discovery by the lenses of infrared cameras or the finely tuned electronic metal detectors of the twentieth century—not to mention the probing minds of psychic investigators. The continual discovery of various ooparts is beginning to bring us closer to our forefathers in a way we never imagined. Studying the various remnants of their technological achievements has added an entirely new dimension to our concept of the lives of these peoples. We are now beginning to learn how they may have lived, and the scattered fragments of their high technology are providing us with little hints that enable us to effect an imaginary reconstruction of some of their accomplishments.

But there is more to be discovered, and the soil that is being turned over by archaeologists with romantic vision is slowly beginning to yield still more of its buried secrets. Archaeology has often been called the "romantic science" because it is a science where dreamers abound. But it is those dreamers who have dug deep into the distant hills and have discovered vast treasures in a thousand different places, testifying not just to the technology but also to the tremendous riches of the nations of old. Archaeologists and their amateur counterparts periodically stumble on some of these secret hiding places; and when they do, others soon join the hunt, spending long hours in smoke-filled rooms, studying ancient maps and translating fragmentary inscriptions, searching for clues to other treasures.

Not long ago a hoard of 139 bronze coins dating back to the reign of Agrippa I (A.D. 37-44) was discovered in an old oil lamp during a series of well-planned excavations of a first-century (A.D.) building at a kibbutz near En-Gedi on the shores of the Dead Sea. The find caused a momentary flurry of excitement. But much more spectacular was the accidental discovery made by a summer volunteer with an archaeological team that was unearthing the walled city of Kurnub some twenty-four miles southeast of Beersheba. There the scraping tools of the amateur archaeologist found, stuffed in a bronze jar hidden in a stairwell, no fewer than 10,000 Roman provincial silver tetradrachms, most of which had been struck during the third century after Christ.

Who hid them, and why?

Only the earth knows, and she doesn't tell—at least not audibly. Our planet is still reluctant to share her treasures, but even so, they are slowly being brought to the surface. The city of Augst in Switzerland was the site of another interesting find in the early 1960s, when excavations with a mechanical shovel uncovered a treasure hoard consisting of almost three hundred pieces of extremely ornate silver, including medals, dishes, eating implements, ingots, and candelabra. Historians who rushed to the scene soon identified the items as having belonged to the Roman emperor Julian the Apostate, who lived in the Roman fort of Augusta Raurica, leaving there in A.D. 351, never to return. It has been speculated that his belongings were buried for safekeeping by loyal servants who then presumably died with the emperor.

It is fascinating to watch both professional and amateur archaeologists in the field with their scraping tools and brushes, probing and cleaning unidentified fragments of something they hope will have historical value. Archaeology as a science isn't all that old. In fact, until the eighteenth century, unearthed artifacts were thought to have been the tools of dwarfs and witches, and it was left to Thomas Jefferson to enter history as the first truly "scientific" archaeologist. It was he who excavated the Indian mounds in his native Virginia, keeping careful notes of his digs and observations—practices which were unheard of up to that time. Napoleon's scientific commission to Egypt and the British and French expeditions to Mesopotamia, on the other hand, were concerned not so much with scientific observation as with grabbing whatever they could and dragging it home as efficiently as possible.

They were merely collecting enterprises. From that point on, the study of archaeology proceeded undisturbed but without specific guidelines for many years. It was not until the beginning of the twentieth century that the subject began to find its own niche in the world of scientific inquiry.

Stimulated by the thoughts of such men as ethnologist Lewis Henry Morgan and Sir Edward Taylor, the early anthropologists entered the scene, reasoning that if there was indeed such a process as biological evolution, then why not consider the possibility of a social evolution as well? Suddenly the search for clues was on, and anthropologists and historians began to examine minutely the soil of the earth, hoping to recover traces of extinct societies.

The advances made since the second world war in the fields of electronics, space exploration and high-resolution photography have introduced new techniques to archaeology and have opened new vistas, greatly expanding the reach of the conventional spade.

Aerial photography has been an accepted tool of the archaeologist for years, and it has proved to be an extremely effective one. From the very moment it was realized that photographs taken from airplanes could sometimes reveal traces of buried structures or roads not visible from the ground, aerial photography was "in." Thanks to new film and filters, aerial pictures can almost be said to talk, for under favorable conditions they present a veritable X ray of topographic features that might otherwise be overlooked.

The photographic capabilities of space satellites which transmit high-resolution pictures of selected target areas back to earth have tied archaeology and photography even closer together. The heart of this process is a new technology called "remote sensing," which means sophisticated interpretation of photographs and other data provided by high-flying aircraft and earth-orbiting satellites. Aerial reconnaissance has several advantages for the archaeologist. It allows scanning for ancient sites much more quickly, less expensively, and on a far greater scale than would ever be possible on the ground. Much of the photography done this way is stereoscopic, providing precise three-dimensional measurement. Computers help manipulate photographs to bring out traces that might escape the human eye. These add up to a new "nondestructive archaeology" which discovers sites but does not disturb them, as opposed to the manual probing of ruins, which leaves them exposed to potential harm. Using photographs such as these, historical detectives have managed to discover hidden structures in Great Britain, lost irrigation canals in Mesopotamia, Etruscan cities in Italy, remains of ancient biblical cities in the Holy Land, and many other centers of antiquity still to be investigated.

But that's only part of the story. Photographs only indicate that there is something underneath the earth's surface. At this point another modern-age tool, the resistivity meter, takes over. With the aerial photographs as a guide, electrodes are hammered into the ground at strategic points, and an electric current is passed through the ground. Buried objects or structures tend to obstruct the expected current flow, and measuring this resistance supplies the field archaeologist with guidelines as to where to dig and possibly what to expect.

The development of the transistor and the subsequent miniaturization of the mine detectors used by the armed forces have led to still another important development—that of scouting for buried metallic objects with the use of metal detectors. Professionals and amateurs alike now comb fields and beaches for buried treasure, and when the original aerial photographs and resistivity soundings are further supported by the insistent beeps of a metal detector, the romance of archaeology evolves into diligently planned activity.

During explorations that were being conducted in Tarquinia in 1958, a geophysical prospecting team found indications of the presence of a great number of what appeared to be tombs in the ancient Etruscan cemetery of Monterozzi, forty miles northwest of Rome. Aerial photography and electrical probing techniques had located several promising spots; and in order to make a detailed inspection of the tombs without disturbing their tranquillity, the experts decided to utilize their newest tool, the "photographic drill."

Developed by Carlo M. Lerici, vice-president of the Lerici Foundation of the Milan Polytechnic Institute, the "drill" consists of a three-inch tube that has been fitted with a tiny Minox camera of the type originally used in wartime espionage. The camera, which is extremely compact and uses a film only slightly larger than regular 8-mm movie film, is mounted behind a window in the tube, while a second window in the tube houses the high-intensity flash unit.

After a hole had been drilled in one of the tombs with an electric earth drill, the tube was slowly lowered into the cavity below. The Etruscan tombs have often been called the "tombs of gold" because of the jewelry and other objects that have been found buried with the dead; and it was with high expectations that Franco Brancaleoni, the leader of the field party, pushed the remote-control button, taking picture after picture. After he had taken twelve shots, turning the camera thirty degrees after each exposure, the entire interior of the tomb had been photographed; then the tube was retracted, leaving only a three-inch hole in the covering rock.

The treasures revealed by the pictures were astounding in many ways, for instead of gold, the camera had photographed a sixth-century B.C. art collection of frescoes of such rare beauty that renowned experts such as Professor Bartoccini and his associate Dr. Mario Moretti of Rome are even today astonished at the quality of this unexpected find.

But while we live in the twentieth century and have access to the newest developments in the field of science in our search for treasure, we are still deeply affected by superstition and by belief in supernatural guidance from one source or another; and thus it was only a matter of time until the psychics would bring their highly controversial talents to bear on the science of archaeology. Using psychic insight is admittedly a rather unorthodox approach to a respected discipline, and because of that it has kicked up a veritable dust storm of debate. In my work as a journalist, I was first confronted with the practice in the early seventies while writing a book about a self-proclaimed psychic, David Bubar.

"My relationship with Ike [Miller] began in the year 1964, when I visited an acquaintance, Dave Early, in Eureka, California," David recalled. "His brother-in-law, Joe Jessel, was reputed to be a faith healer, and desperate people from both the United States and Canada continually sought his help. One such man who was searching for a cure for his arthritis was Ike Miller.

"I fail to recall why Ike happened to be at the Earlys' that day, but I was with him only a few moments when I psychically 'felt' silver all around him. When I told him he grinned, tobacco juice dripping down the corners of his mouth.

" 'I've been a prospector and a jack-of-all-trades most of my life,' he countered proudly. 'I'll be eighty-three on January 24, and you name it and I've been there and done it!'

"I sat down beside the old miner and concentrated on him.

" 'I feel that you have connections with several pieces of property,' I told him, and went on to describe each of them in the minutest detail. 'Two of these lots are in a mountainous region, and I see a heavy silver vein running through the mountain.'

"We talked some more about prospecting in general, and then parted for the evening. I thought our discussion was finished. That is, until he called me a few months later from somewhere in British Columbia.

" 'I've got me some old maps of this mountain terrain up here,' he shouted excitedly over the phone, 'and want to mail them to you. I have a feeling there's a lot of silver up here. Can you take a look at the maps and mark the spots for me?'

"Not long after our conversation, I received the maps. Silver veins ran in all directions . . . With a thick crayon I carefully marked several X's on the maps and mailed them back to him.

"Shortly thereafter I received another phone call from Ike.

" 'Got the maps, David,' he chuckled. 'You must be quite something. Your X's are just about where I had figured the silver must be. What now?'

" 'Jump, Ike! Jump on it!' I said as forcefully as I could. 'There is a lot of silver up there, but you'll be too late if you don't charter a helicopter today—right now—and stake your claim. Tomorrow will be your last chance. Saturday will be too late. File those claims tomorrow or forget it!' "

Without a moment's delay Ike chartered a helicopter, staked his claims and filed them the next day. How fortunate that he did, for the following day headlines screamed about one of the largest silver strikes in British Columbia's history, and precisely in the same area. Within hours eager prospectors were crawling all over the mountains, with their picks and shovels at the ready, staking claims left and right and swearing their choicest oaths when stopped by Ike Miller's claims.

"But that wasn't all. One evening a few short weeks later, as I was having a sandwich with some friends, the phone rang. It was Ike.

" 'I'm rich, David!' he yelled into the phone. 'I've struck it rich! Remember the mountain you said was on one of the claims? Well, it's an artificial mountain. It was a huge pile of silver ore. This pile was formed when overhead buckets from another mining operation passed over this piece of land years ago, sloshing some of the ore from the buckets as they made a sharp turn. In time a huge pile of ore has built up—and now it's mine!'

" 'How high is the pile of ore?' I asked.

" 'About seventy-five thousand tons of it,' Miller replied.

" 'How much do you think it's worth?'

" 'There's over a million dollars' worth of ore lying there, David,' he replied in a hushed tone; and with a voice choking with emotion he added, 'I am rich, David! I am rich! It has finally happened!' "

This occurred back in 1964. It never made the headlines; psychic geology and psychic archaeology didn't make much of an impression in those days. Today, however, things are changing. In a recent article in the January/February 1981 issue, *Science Digest* calls attention to a number of notable cases of psychic archaeology and reports that a Los Angeles–based firm called Mobius used psychics to help them uncover the two-thousand-year-old Ptolemaic ruins of the ancient city of Alexandria in Egypt. The Mobius Group, founded by Stephen A. Schwartz in 1977, is an independent research organization working primarily in the field of applied parapsychology. Beginning in late 1978, after several smaller experiments, Mobius began planning a project which by now has given them a good deal of publicity, most of it favorable. The thrust of the Alexandria Project, as it is known, was to investigate Alexandria's harbor for artifacts dating back to the time of Egypt's Queen Cleopatra. In two separate diving experiments during 1979–80, the thirty-nine-year-old Schwartz and his team of divers found the columns and walls of a large house they believe to be the actual remains of the home of Egypt's Cleopatra, the queen who ensnared Roman emperor Julius Caesar and his general Mark Antony. They also claim to have found the ruins of Mark Antony's palace, known as the Timonium, in nearby waters at a depth of eighteen to twenty-five feet. Other finds by Mobius in the same area include a seven-to-eight-foot stone pharaonic crown which may have been part of a statue of the god Osiris; the body of a small sphinx; and a large temple complex close to the area where Pharos Lighthouse, one of the Seven Wonders of the World, was discovered.

Schwartz's method for locating these hidden objects with the use of psychics is unique. At the start of a project, he mails each psychic on his list a map of the area, together with a list of relevant questions, each one sealed in an envelope. He calls it his "fortune cookie approach." "The psychics get the envelopes, tear them open, read the questions, and respond to them, using whatever approach they find comfortable. While we don't understand a lot of this very well, we do know that we have individuals who work with us regularly and who consistently provide accurate data." The psychics involved in the project circle areas of interest on their map and describe what they "feel" or "see" there. Once all these maps are back at Mobius headquarters, the originals are photocopied and put into a bank. The copies then become the basis for an overlay which shows areas of consensus. It is at this point that the scientists take over from the psychics and put their expertise to work.

Mobius is convinced of the validity of its method, but

all doubts have not been erased from the archaeological community. Robert Bianchi, associate director of Egyptian and classical art of the Brooklyn Museum, is one who doesn't believe in it. "There are bound to be underwater ruins in a place as big as Alexandria," he reasons, "but whether they can be identified is another story." In an interview with the *Los Angeles Times*, Schwartz defended his use of paranormal phenomena. In response to criticism about his Alexandria Project, he said, "There is no question that a great number of scientists don't believe [in the paranormal], find it difficult to understand, or have an emotional position based on no knowledge whatsoever. It is also true that many of the leading scientists in the country not only accept it as reality, but are actively doing research in it.

"Physicists, among others, have taken a close look at paranormal abilities during the last decade. In 1979, nine respected scientists wrote *The Iceland Papers*, detailing physical experiments on psychics. In the book, Brian D. Josephson, Nobel laureate of physics at Cambridge University, wrote, 'In recent years, a number of reputable scientists have entered the field [of paranormal research] with expert knowledge of how to perform good experiments . . . still it appears that the phenomena occur.' "

Controversial? Most definitely. But Mobius is not the only one to claim that psychics have the inside track.

Half a world away in Arizona, Jeffrey D. Goodman, a professional archaeologist, claims that it was a psychic who led him to a site in the mountains near Flagstaff that may contain 100,000-year-old human artifacts, even though his training has taught him that *Homo sapiens* did not appear on the world scene until approximately 40,000 years ago—though even that is one hundred percent speculation. What this all means is that psychic investigators are now beginning to supply information that may be too startling even to the individuals who hired them for their "expertise." Thus, Goodman's findings have not solved a problem but have merely added fuel to the controversy concerning psychic archaeology.

Comments Kenneth L. Feder of Central Connecticut State College,

"Psychic archaeologists don't want to play by the same rules that scientists play by. They don't set out to test their hypotheses; they set out to prove them."

But is that so bad? No matter which technique or discovery method is used to retrieve the treasures tucked away deep within the folds of Mother Earth, whether it be a crude spade, satellite photography, current resistivity, metal detectors or psychic visions, discovering the undiscovered is the ultimate aim, and this aim has become one of this century's major preoccupations. Professionals are now joined by the amateurs with their costly detection equipment and inventive methods, which will only add to the controversy of who's right and who's wrong; but let's hope this will not distract either group from their goal. Whatever they find will undoubtedly further our understanding of the customs, development, technical know-how and riches of the many nations whose memories and treasures were inadvertently trampled underfoot.

CHAPTER 2

The Elusive Treasures of the Holy Land

The year was 1947—a good year for dreamers.

It was my first year in college, and the two professions I wanted most of all to pursue were archaeology and journalism, yet I didn't see how I could effectively prepare for both of them at the same time. But this dilemma certainly did not prevent me from dreaming. I was eager to try my wings, and when I received an invitation to spend part of my summer as part of a team who traversed the country raising money to outfit an expedition to locate the legendary Ark of Noah, plus the Golden Ark of the Covenant *and* the temple treasures of Solomon's Temple, I dreamed loud and clear. "When do we start?"

Two days later we were on our way in a long black twelve-cylinder Pierce-Arrow: David Greene, Milton St. John (a silver-maned gentle-faced retired minister) and I. Our efforts consisted of making a grand tour of five thousand miles, touching base with possible financiers and with other dreamers like us. But while we aroused much interest in the project, backers were few; and at the end of the summer we found ourselves back in Hollywood, California, an expensive experience wiser.

Yet somehow the dream remained very much alive

throughout the numerous Noah's Ark expeditions in which I became involved over the years, although the Golden Ark of Solomon's Temple and the whereabouts of the vast temple treasures that were hidden from the Babylonians before they took Jerusalem in 586 B.C. remained as elusive as ever. Still concealed also were the temple treasures of the Second Temple and the gold and silver of Jerusalem's nobility that was hurriedly smuggled out of the holy city through secret passages and buried throughout Palestine during the frightening days of the Roman encirclement of the city in A.D. 70.

To those knowledgeable about the Middle East, it is no secret that the Holy Land in particular is a vast depository of treasure which has been hidden for thousands of years. The barren yellowish hills of the land are honeycombed with innumerable caves, their entrances coarsely blocked either by men or by natural causes, carefully hiding hoards of precious metals, jars of coins, and glittering stones placed there by trembling hands. Yet aside from an occasional assortment of gold ornaments found in a newly discovered tomb or a handful of coins found scattered among the potsherds, the rumored treasures of the ancients still lie hidden, taking shape only as they are discussed over the smoldering campfires of the Bedouins or the young Israelis who yearn for their legendary pot of gold.

But nothing ever remains unchanged. For while we were roaming around the United States in search of funds for expeditions, a young Arab goatherd named Mohammed accidentally stumbled on a cache of ancient manuscripts near a dried-out riverbed known as the Wadi Qumran along the rocky shores of the Dead Sea not far from the old city of Jericho. And although he was totally unaware of the value of his extraordinary discovery at the time, it ultimately became one of the most significant finds in archaeological history. Biblical scholars from all parts of the world soon converged on Jerusalem, scaling the foot-worn steps of the Palestine Archaeological Museum to examine these remarkable scrolls with the hope of assisting in their translations.

Realizing that this fortuitous discovery could mark the beginning of a highly lucrative business, other Arabs in the Qumran area soon began to probe every known cave for possible artifacts; and within weeks cave after cave succumbed to the crowbars and pickaxes of the untrained but eager scavengers.

Considerable concern was felt in scientific circles, but it was not until 1952 that a group of worried archaeologists finally took it upon themselves to make one last concerted effort to search the area where the scrolls had been discovered in 1947; and on March 4 their diligence was finally rewarded. While stumbling along near the bottom of a steep cliff, they suddenly caught sight of a number of potsherds that had accumulated among the crumbling rocks. When they knelt down to examine them, they began to notice small irregularly torn fragments of parchment. Excitedly their hands reached out to claw at the rocky dirt that had piled up against the cliff, and within minutes the formerly forbidding rock face opened up, revealing the narrow entrance to a cave.

Nervous excitement spread among the members of the search party as they enlarged the cave opening and carefully moved in with their cameras, notebooks, measuring tapes, small shovels and brushes. It was obvious, however, that the ravages of time plus generations of vermin and insects had destroyed much of what had been left in the cave for safekeeping. Just when it began to appear that Cave #3—as it was already being called—would take its place in history as a total disappointment, one of the archaeologists noticed two dust-covered objects, one piled on top of the other, lying against the far wall. Closer examination revealed that although they bore no resemblance to ordinary scrolls—they were cylindrical in shape and were cast from metal—their oxidized surfaces revealed the chisel marks of ancient writing. To avoid further damage to the scrolls, careful hands lifted them from their resting place and sprayed them with a celluloid solution before taking them to Dr. Joseph Saad at the Jerusalem Archaeological Museum. Once placed on the examining table and exposed to the bright lights and curious eyes of the experts, the scrolls began to release the first of their many secrets. It was soon apparent that the two scrolls had been cut from one single sheet of copper alloy, which in its original shape had been about one foot wide and eight feet in length. A line of fragmented rivets along one of the edges corresponded with a row of holes on the edge of the other scroll, indicating that they had indeed been part of the same sheet of metal.

Lying on a soft bed of cotton, protected from eager fingers by a layer of thick glass, they resumed their age-old rest, but this time in the Jerusalem Museum. What were they? What did they signify? Who had written them? What was the message on the scrolls? From the very moment they were discovered they became the central object of endless guesswork and many hypotheses, but no one really knew the answers, nor did anyone dare take the responsibility for attempting to unroll the brittle scrolls.

It was while they were still locked up in this fashion that I first saw the copper scrolls. As I was escorted through the Museum by Dr. Saad, I remember staring at them in amazement, wondering what those little indentations might have to tell us.

Of course, I was not the only visitor who wondered about the scrolls' meaning; and I was only one of many who could not be of any help in their translation. Fortunately, there were others whose interest and abilities went much deeper than those of a visiting journalist. A German

professor, K. G. Kuhn, was one of them. Carefully examining the scrolls under glass and bringing his knowledge of
ancient Hebrew to bear in his attempt to translate the
inscriptions, he concluded that the scrolls contained a
detailed list of hidden treasure. He had been able to separate and identify the words "gold," "silver," "buried,"
and "cubit," and to him this was more than sufficient to
justify his conclusion.

Scientists can be extremely critical and jealous of one
another when it comes to an evaluation of material that
has not been made available to everyone, or which the dis-
coverers themselves have not as yet been able to identify
or translate. Professor Kuhn's idea that the mysterious
copper scrolls were actually a sort of treasure inventory
raised learned eyebrows and quickly caused an avalanche
of critical comment. But very little was done at the time to
contradict his conclusion. In fact, very little could be
done—and Professor Kuhn knew it—for to the despair of
the scholars entrusted with the problem of translating the
scrolls' inscriptions, oxidation had made the metal too
dangerously brittle to handle, and any attempt to unroll
the scrolls was out of the question. It had already been
decided to take the problem of preservation out of the
hands of the biblical scholars, for unless the chemists and
physicists could find a way to unroll them and thus to
expose the entire text to scrutiny, their message would be
forever lost. And while the scrolls rested in their glass display case for another three and a half years, keen minds
were busy deliberating on a way to unravel the mystery of
Cave #3.

Johns Hopkins University was the first to come up with
a possible solution. In a unique experiment they analyzed
a fragment of the copper of the scroll in order to determine its exact alloy. Next they made up a copper alloy of
the exact formula and rolled it to the same thickness, after
which they subjected it to artificial oxidation, transform-

ing it to nearly the same state as the original copper scrolls. After countless experiments, a process was developed that would return the oxidized copper back to its pristine condition. It had been a painstaking procedure but a successful one.

However, the transatlantic phone call announcing the achievement came too late. Not knowing how long it might take Johns Hopkins to run through all its available options, American scholars had finally worked out an agreement with the Jordanian authorities to have one of the scrolls turned over to Manchester University in England, where an attempt would be made to cut the scroll into strips. The job was assigned to Professor H. Wright Baker of the University's College, who decided to use a homemade contraption of rather primitive construction: a saw disk fine enough to cut incisions of six one-thousandths of an inch in thickness.

When the first strip was cut and the dust had been brushed off, the unmistakable Hebrew words stood out, literally begging for translation; and before the first full day was over, Professor Kuhn's early judgment of the scrolls' being treasure lists was more than vindicated. *The copper scrolls were indeed lists of hidden treasure, with detailed guidelines pointing the way to caches of gold and silver in bullion, ornaments, temple vessels, coins, trays and cups in such huge quantities that the translators stood aghast.*

As soon as they were informed that the first scroll had been cut successfully, the Jordanian authorities indicated their willingness to ship the second one to Manchester for similar treatment. When both of the scrolls had finally been cut with Professor Baker's saw, the corroded material revealed no fewer than twelve well-separated columns of ancient Hebrew text, each line filled with intricate details of and directions for finding hidden treasures in and around the city of Old Jerusalem and in the moun-

tainous area along the shores of the Dead Sea and near
the city of Jericho. The scrolls were totally devoid of any
historical references or any reasons why the treasures were
being hidden; but the very locations and the often hurried
descriptions of the various hiding places betrayed the terror of those who had hidden their fortune and bore wit-
ness to their desperate efforts to find secure places to hide
the personal and temple treasures from the ruthless invaders who were closing in on them.

The translation that began the first day after the cutting
has led to a total decipherment of both scrolls; but even
though two translations have already been published,
there is still serious doubt among scholars concerning
their accuracy. The two versions differ so drastically in
almost every line that a simple comparison often increases
rather than decreases the problem of understanding the
real meaning of the text. For our purpose we have not
only taken a look at the two translations but have also
merged their essence with the views of other Hebrew
scholars in order to produce something that will portray
at least the basic meaning of the secrets of the scrolls.

Yet even if all the scholars had agreed on one translation, it would not bring us closer to solving the mystery of
the scrolls, for their origin and the time at which the various treasures were hidden is still shrouded in a veil of
uncertainty.

Some archaeologists have proposed that they are nothing more than the records of the Qumran community's
possessions and were concealed just prior to the Romans'
advance on their "monastery" around A.D. 68. However,
the Essenes who lived in Qumran were an ascetic people,
and a treasure of this magnitude would have been totally
disproportionate to their way of life. It has also been suggested that the treasures belonged to the Second Temple,
that they were committed to the Qumran community in a
last desperate attempt to keep them safe from the assault-

ing Romans when they sacked the temple. Flavius Josephus, the famed historian of antiquity, however, maintains that the treasure was not removed but was still in the temple when it fell to the Romans in A.D. 70. If that is true, then the Essenes of Qumran could not have had it in their possession, for their stronghold had already been overrun by the Romans in 68, two years earlier!

But there is a still more plausible theory which makes finding the treasure even more desirable. *Many scholars now believe that it was part of the enormous treasure of the Temple of Solomon, removed from Jerusalem just before King Nebuchadnezzar's army forced its way into the city in 586 B.C.*

Which one is true? Is it possible that a key to the fabulous wealth of the world's wisest king has actually been uncovered? Unfortunately, the mystery of the scrolls is like a gigantic puzzle most of whose pieces have been forever lost.

It has often been said that a treasure hunt is not complete without a map, and while the treasure list and the descriptions given on the scrolls will not help us create a treasure map in the true sense of the word, by following the various directions and locations as indicated in the scrolls the modern treasure hunter will find himself roaming over much of the Holy Land, thereby creating a treasure map of his own. But he must be prepared to traverse a lot of land, for wherever nations were subjugated by pagans, there is hidden treasure to be found; and in antiquity the pagans were everywhere.

Another fascinating aspect of the old copper scrolls is that they not only describe the amount and type of treasure hidden at a given location, but provide detailed descriptions of the hiding places as well. This advantage, however, has been countered by time. The accumulation of years has a tendency to obliterate many of the old landmarks left by our forefathers, and this same phenomenon has put its mark on the Holy Land. Even though the modern treasure hunter may be equipped with an accurate translation of the scrolls and may bring along his useful spade, tape measure, compass and metal detector, he will need a supernatural degree of wisdom in addition to perseverance in his search for the Jewish treasure, for the landmarks that were pinpointed in the copper scrolls have been changed.

I have no doubt that the treasure is there somewhere, but the mystery of the scrolls has added an extra dimension to the search.

The sixty-one hiding places listed in the twelve columns of the scrolls are—in free translation—described as follows:

(1) There is a money chest in the fortress in the Vale of Anchor, containing a weight of *seventeen talents,* and it is hidden forty cubits deep under the steps of the eastern entrance.

(2) *Light bars of gold* have been hidden in the third course of stones in the monument on top of the sepulchre.

(3) *Nine hundred talents* are hidden in a hole in the beginning of the upper opening in the plaster of the floor of the great cistern in the Court of Peristyle.

(4) In the trough of the Place of the Basin are *tithe vessels,* and amphorae and second tithes are hidden (all the way) from the mouth to the opening and in the bottom of the water pipe in the direction of the chiseled immersion pool located six cubits from the north.

(5) In the left-hand side going up the Staircase of Refuse, at the height of three cubits from the floor, are *forty talents of silver* hidden.

(6) *Forty talents* are under the steps of the salt pit.

(7) *Sixty-five bars of gold* are hidden in the Platform of the Chain in the cellar of the Old House of Tribute.

(8) In a barrel in the underground passage in the Court are hidden *seventy talents* of silver and a measure of untithed goods.

(9) *Six hundred pitchers of silver* are hidden in a spur of rock in the cistern under the east wall under the Great Threshold.

(10) In the cistern which is nineteen cubits before the eastern gateway are vessels containing *ten talents.*

(11) *Twenty-two talents* are buried at a depth of one cubit in a hole in the northern corner of the pool which is in the east.

(12) *Gold and silver vessels for tithe, sprinkling basins, cups, sacrificial bowls, and libation vessels* for a total of six hundred and nine are hidden at a depth of six cubits under the southern corner of the Court.

(13) Under the other eastern corner are *forty talents of silver* buried at sixteen cubits.

(14) *Tithe vessels and garments* are hidden in the pit of . . . . Its entrance to it is under the western corner.

(15) *Thirteen talents* are hidden under the corpse which is in the tomb with the shaft leading to the north.

(16) . . . . *talents* are hidden in a hole in the northern pillar in the Great Cistern.

(17) In a chest in the water conduit which enters the . . . . as you go into . . . . are *forty talents of silver* in a chest.

(18) In the middle of the two oil presses that are in the Vale of Anchor, buried at a depth of three cubits, are *two pots filled with silver.*

(19) *Two hundred talents of silver* are hidden in the clay pit at the bottom of the winepress.

(20) In the eastern pit in the north have *seventy talents of silver* been hidden.

(21) In the water that is in the Valley of Secacah are *three talents of silver* buried at a depth of one cubit.

(22) *Seven talents of silver* are hidden at a depth of three

cubits under the great basin at the beginning of the water channel which enters Secacah from the north.

(23) In a crack in the plaster of Solomon's Pool in Secacah are *tithe vessels containing coins with images.*

(24) *Thirteen talents* are buried at a depth of three cubits at a distance of sixty cubits from Solomon's trench in the direction of the great watchtower.

(25) In the tomb in the Wadi Kippa along the eastern road to Secacah are *thirty-two talents* buried at a depth of seven cubits.

(26) *A pitcher with a scroll and under it forty-two talents* are buried at three cubits in the room of the platform of the Double Gate facing east.

(27) *Twenty-one talents* are buried at a depth of nine cubits in the inner room of the corner of the eastern watchtower.

(28) *Nine talents* are hidden at a depth of twelve cubits at the western side of the Tomb of the Queen.

(29) In the dam-sluice in the Bridge of the Priest are *nine talents.*

(30) In the water pipe of . . . . the northern pool . . . . on the left side of it at a distance of twenty cubits are *four hundred talents.*

(31) *Six pitchers of silver* are buried at a depth of six cubits in the inner room which is next to the cool room of the Summer House.

(32) *Twenty-two talents* are buried at seven cubits in a hole under the eastern corner of the wide platform.

(33) *Eighty talents of gold* are buried in two pitchers near the opening of the drainpipe three cubits toward the overflow tank.

(34) *Tithe jars with scrolls hidden amongst the jars* are in the water channel which is on the eastern path to the treasury.

(35) *Seventeen talents of silver and gold* are buried at a

depth of seventeen cubits in the middle of the Circle on the Stone in the Outer Valley.

(36) In the dam sluice at the mouth of the Kidron Valley are *seven* talents buried at a depth of three cubits.

(37) . . . . in the stubble field of the Shaveh, facing southwest . . . .

(38) In the drain of the irrigation pool of the Shavez are *seventy talents* of silver buried at a depth of eleven cubits.

(39) In the gutter at the bottom of the water tank, concealed in the plaster lining of the side, are *four staters.*

(40) *Twenty-four talents* are buried at a depth of eight and a half cubits in the underground passage facing east of the Second Enclosure.

(41) *Twenty-two talents* have been buried in the plaster at a depth of sixteen cubits in the underground room of the Holies in the passage facing south.

(42) In the "shute" is *silver from the consecrated offerings.*

(43) *Nine talents* have been hidden in the drainpipe used to let water run to the basin of the drain, at a distance of seven cubits from the open area toward the outlet.

(44) *Consecrated offerings* have been hidden in the tomb in the north at the beginning of the ravine of the Place of Palms at the Outlet of the Valley of PL.

(45) In the southern opening in the second story in the drain of the stronghold of Senaah are *nine talents* hidden.

(46) In the cistern of the Ravine of the Deep which gets its water from the Great Wadi are *twelve talents* in the floor.

(47) As you enter the reservoir in Beth Kerem, on the left, at a distance of ten cubits, are *sixty-two talents of silver.*

(48) *Three hundred talents of gold and ten serving vessels* are hidden behind the stone stopper of two cubits in diameter which is in the western side of the tank of the olive press.

(49) On the western side of the Monument of Absalom at a depth of twelve cubits are *eighty talents* buried.

(50) Under the drain of the pool of the Bathhouse with running water are *seventeen talents*.

(51) Tithe vessels containing coins with images are in the four inner corner buttresses.

(52) *Vessels for tithe sweepings, spoiled tithes, and coins with images* are buried below the south corner of the porch of the Tomb of Zadok under the entrance platform.

(53) Under the great sealing stone on the cliff side facing west of the Garden of Zadok in the entrance to the tomb are *consecrated offerings*.

(54) In the grave itself under the paving stones are *forty talents*.

(55) *Vessels for tithe or tithe refuse and coins with images* are buried in the graves of the common people who died free of obligations.

(56) As you go into the House with the Two Pools, from the direction of the settling basin are *vessels for liquid tithe and degenerated tithe and coins with images*.

(57) *Nine hundred talents of gold and sixty talents in small jugs* have been thrown into the cut-out rooms of the western tomb. The entrance to the tomb is from the west. Another *forty-two talents* are hidden under the sill of the tomb chamber.

(58) Under the entrance of the upper pit in Mount Gerizim is a chest with *sixty talents of silver*.

(59) In the mouth of the well of the Temple are *vessels of silver and gold for tithe and money totaling six hundred talents*.

(60) In the Great Drain of the Basin are instruments of the House of the Basin for a total of *seventy-one talents and twenty minas.*

(61) In the pit to the north in a hole with an opening to the north buried at the opening is a copy of this document with an explanation and measurements and inventory of everything.

To ascertain the total amount of treasure referred to in the scrolls, I have tallied the precious metals in much the same way as John Marco Allegro has done in his remarkable book, *The Treasure of the Copper Scrolls.* After rechecking his figures, I have reached basically the same conclusion; i.e., that the total amount of treasure hidden is:

Gold	1,280	talents
	65	bars
Silver	3,282	talents
	20	minas
	4	staters
	608	pitchers containing silver
Vessels of silver and gold	619	

There is no agreement whatsoever among biblical scholars as to the exact weight of the talent in biblical times, but the *New Oxford Annotated Bible* gives it the equivalent of 75.558 U.S. pounds, while the average bar of gold is standardized at 32 ounces. With these figures as a basis, a few quick calculations will show that the total amount of gold listed comes to 96,844.24 pounds, which if sold at the average market value of U.S. $500 per ounce comes to $774,753,920.

The value of the buried silver is equally impressive. There we have a total of 338,006.59 pounds, which at the average current market value of U.S. $9 per ounce comes to $48,672,948. Add to this U.S. $1,000 for each one of the 608 pitchers containing silver coins and perhaps another $1,000 for each one of the 619 silver and gold vessels, and we arrive at the staggering sum of $826,093,868.00: not a small treasure by any standard!

The question, however, is: How do we find it—or even a part of it? In searching for treasure in Israel, there are several important points to consider.

1) No excavations for archaeological or geological purposes are permitted without specific permission from the government. If granted, the permit is usually limited to a certain number of days, and often a specific number of hours per day. It may name Israeli representatives who have been selected to accompany the party for the duration of their investigation. In addition, permits are usually granted only to scientists connected with an internationally recognized institute of higher education or a museum. These conditions, of course, severely curtail the amateur archaeologist's activities and may force him to carry out his hobby in Israel covertly.

2) Ancient cities and towns have simply vanished from the map without leaving so much as a trace. Still others have been razed to the ground, their rubble serving as the foundation for other villages with new names. Ofttimes, inhabitants of the former towns, having escaped invasion or natural disasters, built new settlements on other locations, taking the names of the old towns with them and using them for new sites. In some cases tradition has preserved both names and sites; but where traditional descriptions have taken the place of actual place names, the locations of the treasure sites have been lost with the changing times.

Because of factors such as these, many of the locations mentioned on the treasure list of the scrolls will never be found, for time has obliterated too many important landmarks. There are, nevertheless, a number of sites that can be directly pinpointed through the use of biblical references and Jewish history.

For the sake of the twentieth-century treasure hunter, let's single out a number of hiding places that have been well described and see how close we can get to them.

The first four lines of the scroll's list indicate that seventeen talents were hidden in a money chest that was buried at a depth of forty cubits under the steps of the eastern entrance to the fortress in the Vale of Anchor.

Question: Where is the Vale of Anchor? There are a number of references to the Vale of Anchor in the book of Joshua, and from these references Old Testament scholars have deduced that the valley is the five-mile plateau that is also known under the name of Buquei'a, a strip of agricultural land that runs above the cliffs of Qumran. But where and how does one find *the* fortress in a valley that is that long and that old?

History has the answer, for even though the area is literally dotted with remains of old fortifications and primitive strongholds, no spot has been so important as the fortified conical hill on the western edge of the Vale, now known as Khirbat Mird. For years it has been known as Hyrcania, named after John Hyrcanus, the Jewish priest-king (135–104 B.C.) who built a castle fortress on the hill. In later years the ruins of the fortress became the building blocks for a small monastery. There is no doubt that the correct Vale of Anchor has been located, and so has the fortress. Now all that remains is the money chest with its 1284.486 pounds of silver (seventeen talents), and at least one of the mysterious treasures of the copper scrolls will have been found!

But this is where the hard part comes in. Locating the Vale and the right fortress was easy compared with finding the exact spot where the treasure was left. No one knows the outline of the basic foundation of the ancient fortress; and without knowing the precise location of the eastern entrance, how can one attempt to find the remains of its seventeen steps under which the money chest was hidden? Mountains of sand cover the ruins, as they have done for generations, and only a major excavation would offer any hope of finding the outlines of the actual foundation of the fortress.

But the list has many more treasure locations to choose from. Six of the sixty-one treasure spots refer to valuables hidden in various locations in Secacah. It places silver talents buried under a great basin, in the plaster at Solomon's Pool, near a trench, and in a tomb, in wording sufficiently clear so that a good treasure hunter might be able to locate some if not all—provided that Secacah itself can first be found.

John Marco Allegro again has done some remarkable Old Testament detective work in locating this old settlement. His painstaking comparison of the ancient Hebrew text with traditional names around the Dead Sea and his matching of Old Testament references led him to conclude that "the only real possibility for our Secacah is Khirbat Qumran itself, the site of the Essene monastery. Not only do the details of the scroll's description coincide remarkably well with what we find in the excavated settlement; but it has recently been shown that the Essenes built their desert home on much earlier remains, dating from Old Testament times." A little further on he adds a statement of great significance to those treasure hunters who might like to investigate the whereabouts of the thirty-two talents (2417.9) pounds of silver hidden in the tomb in the Wadi Kippa. "The eastern road to Secacah," he points out, referring to item 25 on our list, "must be the track leading to the monastery plateau from the coast, parallel with the last furlongs of the Wadi Qumran."

On several occasions, while on magazine assignments as a member of various archaeological expeditions into

Israel and specifically the Dead Sea area, I have checked the Wadi Qumran and searched for tombs. The territory appears raw and untouched, yet I have been assured that several ancient gravesites have been uncovered in its immediate vicinity. Has the wadi perhaps changed its course just enough during the past two and a half thousand years to throw the modern investigator completely off the track? Or is it possible that the river's course has not changed but the tomb's superstructure has succumbed to the ravages of time, and that the tomb and the silver treasure are still in relatively the same position, just waiting to be discovered? It undoubtedly warrants a thorough investigation, for even if the tomb in the wadi should be found to be of no great archaeological significance, the possibility of finding its hidden treasure of nearly $350,000 in silver should at least make it a worthwhile adventure.

The Monument of Absalom is another location that the scrolls have singled out as a possible target for a treasure hunt, for it is there, it states, that eighty talents of silver have been buried at a depth of twelve cubits. The current market value of that much silver is approximately $870,000, and for those who like to gamble on a long shot, this might be just the one to tackle!

But again, here is a problem. No one really knows for sure whether the tomb in Jerusalem's Kidron Valley known as Absalom's Tomb is actually the tomb erected for or by the son of David. Various traditions support the position that the present tomb dates back only to the first century before Christ, while other accounts take it back much further. The rocks immediately surrounding the tomb do not show any evidence of a shaft or a tunnel in which eighty talents of silver could have been hidden, but at a distance of sixteen yards from the tomb on the western side is an opening to a cistern which is said to be more than ten cubits deep and is said to run in the direction of

the tomb. The shaft itself is empty, but is it possible that
the treasure is hidden somewhere at the end of the shaft?

Item number 48 on the list mentions three hundred talents of gold and ten serving vessels that were carefully
concealed behind the stopper of an olive press but without
any further identification. Only by connecting it to a previously mentioned hiding place (item 47) do we find a possible lead, for there reference is made to a reservoir which
is in Beth Kerem. A literal translation of Beth Kerem is
"Place of the Vineyard" and consequently a logical location for an olive- or winepress. In Jeremiah 6:1, the
prophet places it to the south of Jerusalem, while still others identify it with the present-day 'Ain Karim. It has also
been rumored that there might be a connection between
the hiding place and the olive press that used to be in the
Garden of Gethsemane. There are indeed several alterna-
tives—but here, too, the monetary value of the hidden
treasure will more than compensate the seeker for
tediously combing through ancient records and piles of
rubble, for, if successful, he will be rewarded with a treasure worth $181,339,200.

For those well acquainted with Jerusalem, treasure spot
number 26 should be most familiar, for it is supposed to
be in the platform of the Double Gate, also known as the
Golden Gate, that forty-two talents of silver ($253,874.88)
have been hidden. The present gate was constructed six
centuries *after* Christ, but it was very probably rebuilt in
much the same fashion as the original gate, only without a
platform or an inner room in which the treasure could be
hidden. The gate is deeply immersed in rabbinic tradition,
and the many secrets that are connected with its history
as well as the size and shape of the original platform are
known only from Jewish literature. No one knows
whether the men who built the new gate preserved the old
inner chamber or the platform of the old gate. Only a
full-scale archaeological excavation will answer that question to everyone's satisfaction. But that will probably

never happen, for Jerusalem's Arab population regards the area in front of the gate as their sacred burial ground, and any excavation would undoubtedly result in immediate reprisals.

Where does this leave the modern treasure hunter and his unfulfilled dreams of finding the almost one billion dollars' worth of gold and silver that lies hidden somewhere in the Holy Land? In most areas he will be allowed to wander freely and be allowed to work quietly; he will remain undisturbed as long as no one knows what he is digging for. Many of the places mentioned on the corroded treasure list have been pinpointed with a fair degree of accuracy now by Old Testament scholars—but that is usually as far as their interest goes. Modern treasure hunting has become a field for specialists, for men with gold fever, resistivity meters and metal detectors—not necessarily the customary tools of the conventional archaeologist or Old Testament scholar. The fascination of the copper scrolls has by now created a gold fever with a quality all its own. A search for the scrolls' treasures possesses all the elements needed to make the job a very special one indeed. Every one of the clues on the crumbling treasure list presents its own unique set of identification problems, complicated by the shifting sands of time, and calls for a detailed background study of each location before any real fieldwork can be undertaken.

The scrolls of Cave #3 have made the Holy Land as promising a place for treasure hunters as the offshore areas of the Caribbean, even though the techniques employed will be quite different. Will anyone succeed in forcing ancient Israel to yield any of her secret treasures? Only time and luck will tell.

The Ark of the Covenant

No longer are the barren hills and the desolate windswept ruins of the Holy Land regarded merely as picturesque scenery. The knowledge that somewhere within the sandy crevices of the rocks, behind some crumbling old plaster and in unknown water conduits, are caches of treasure totaling close to one billion dollars has made even the most casual outing a subconscious exploration trip. People—natives and tourists alike—are now beginning to scout the land for treasure and are eagerly combing the ruins and steep cliffs of dried-out riverbeds with whatever tools are at their disposal. And the fever continues to rise with the fluctuating price of gold.

Seldom, however, is any serious consideration given to a search for the greatest hidden treasure of all—the golden Ark of the Covenant. In fact, not only is the elusive treasure of religious and historical significance to both Jews and Christians, but its monetary value far will exceed the riches found in King Tut's tomb.

The Ark of the Covenant first appeared in history as *the* central object of religious veneration in the Most Holy Place of the Sanctuary of Israel's tabernacle after the Jews departed Egypt on their way to the Promised Land. It was fashioned by Jewish craftsmen from gold the Jews had carried with them from their land of bondage, and in it Moses placed the Ten Commandments as they were given to him on Mount Sinai.

The ark was a box constructed of acacia wood, four feet four inches long and two feet seven inches in both breadth and height, overlaid inside and out with pure gold. Two golden rings on each side at the bottom enabled the ark to be carried on two poles. On the solid-gold lid stood two golden fifteen-foot-tall cherubim carved in olive wood and garbed in thick oakleaf, their outstretched wings spanning the twenty-five-foot innermost chamber of the Sanctuary and hovering over the Holy Ark.

Even without its religious significance, the ark was certainly an object worthy of reverence and admiration, but to many its splendor could not compare with the magnifi-

An artist's conception of the Ark of the Covenant.

cence of the actual Temple of Solomon in which the ark
finally found a resting place.

Israel experienced a tumultuous growth between 1000
and 920 B.C. during the reigns of King David and King
Solomon. Its mighty armies and commercial power
became the envy of the surrounding nations, and the
Israelites exulted in having a united country and control
of the trade routes necessary to enrich themselves beyond
measure. During this time in history ancient Israel was
rich, fabulously rich, in both gold and silver. In fact, the
Bible tells us that King David contributed 3,000 talents
of gold from the land of Ophir to the building of the
temple. Figuring one talent at the equivalent of 75.558
pounds with 16 ounces to the pound and gold at an
approximate price of U.S. $500 per ounce, David's con-
tribution to the building of the temple alone was worth
$1,813,392,000. Other biblical passages inform us that
Solomon built a fleet of ships which, under the command of King Hiram of Tyre, left the port of Ezion-
Geber on a journey to Ophir and returned with another
420 talents of gold.

According to the Bible account, David's son Solomon,
who built the Temple, had extraordinary amounts of gold
available to him. In addition to Hiram's fleet, Solomon
had another fleet at his disposal, the ships of Tarshish,
which brought him a shipment of gold once every three
years. The altar, the inner sanctuary, and even the floors
of Solomon's Temple were overlaid with gold. The tables
and lampstands and all the sacred vessels in the temple
were made of pure gold—an element so plentiful that
King Solomon overlaid his throne with it, ordered five
hundred shields to be made from it, and even used it for
his drinking cups. According to the biblical book of
Kings, the weight in gold that came to Solomon in one
year amounted to 50,322 pounds (666 talents), which did
not include the gold offered to him by traders and other

rulers who visited his kingdom, such as the Queen of Sheba, who presented him with a gift of 120 talents.

Thus it is no wonder that gold was so lavishly used in the construction of the Temple, which was started in the fourth year of Solomon's reign in 966 B.C. It was a painstaking task, for the dimensions and details are traditionally believed to have been dictated to the king by Jehovah, and to please his God, Solomon spared neither effort nor riches. It has now been estimated that the value of the total amount of gold used in the construction of the temple and its contents was in excess of four billion dollars at current rates of exchange. A truly incredible amount in our day, but even more staggering among the nations of old.

Ever since scholars began to study the issues related to the vast fortune of King Solomon, several important questions have troubled them. They wonder where the legendary land of Ophir really was, and what ever happened to all that gold?

The *Biblical Archaeology Review* in its September 1977 issue discussed the work of a U.S. Geological Survey team in Arabia.

"In the last year, the U.S. Geological Survey announced that they have found King Solomon's mines at Mahd adh Dhahab, an ancient mine in central Saudi Arabia between Mecca and Medina. The *New York Times* quoted Dr. Robert Luce, one of the geologists who was part of the American-Saudi team exploring the area, as saying, 'Our investigations have confirmed that the old mine could have been as rich as described in biblical accounts and, indeed, is a logical candidate to be the lost Ophir . . . . King Solomon's mines are no longer lost.' "

And the remainder of the article supported his statement with details of the find. Other investigations which have been conducted since that time have fully upheld the conclusion of Dr. Luce. His report, however, was only partially original, for in 1932 an American mining engineer named Karl Twitchell explored the country's mining resources at the request of King Ibn Saud and reached basically the same conclusion at the end of his investigation.

Thus with one of the possible sources of King Solomon's gold having been identified, what ultimately happened to that vast fortune in gold that was used in the Israelite Kingdom between 1000 and 920 before Christ?

The copper scrolls have already shed much light on what happened to at least one billion dollars' worth of it, and perhaps another billion was removed by the Babylonian war machine that eventually crushed Jerusalem's resistance after shaking its walls for eighteen long months with battering rams and siege machines until the city fell in 587 B.C. The bloody slaughter that followed took the lives of the children of King Zedekiah, along with thousands of others. The Babylonians plundered and sacked the city ruthlessly, stripping the royal palace and the temple of the remaining treasures and golden vessels, and ended their frenzy by setting the city aflame. With the murder of the royal family and the removal of the now helpless and blinded King Zedekiah to Babylon, Israel's powerful adversary Nebuchadnezzar had effectively eradicated the House of David, which had reigned without interruption for four hundred years.

The city was destroyed.

The royal family was murdered and the king blinded and taken into exile.

The temple was plundered, and the remaining sacrificial vessels were taken.

But where was the Ark of the Covenant?

While there are sufficient historical references in II Kings 25, Daniel 5, and II Chronicles 36 that Nebuchadnezzar indeed carried off the temple treasures, there is not an accurate listing of the stolen items. A detailed account can, however, be found in the historical book of Ezra at 1:9–11, where Nebuchadnezzar's booty is described as follows:

"And this is the number of them: thirty chargers of gold, a thousand chargers of silver, nine and twenty knives.

"Thirty basins of gold, silver basins of a second sort four hundred and ten, and other vessels a thousand.

"All the vessels of gold and of silver were five thousand and four hundred."

But still—no Ark of the Covenant.

It is at this point in ancient history that the golden Ark of the Covenant totally vanishes from the accepted historical record. The Bible simply no longer refers to it. But history does not leave us completely uninformed. The Apocrypha, the so-called hidden books that have never truly found a fitting place within the biblical canon by the Christian Church, provide us with a glimmer as to what may have happened to it just prior to the Babylonian sacking of the temple.

Maccabees 2:4–8 contains the following passage:

"Further, this document records that, prompted by a divine message, the prophet gave orders that the Tent of the Meeting and the Ark should go with him. Then he went away to the mountain from the top of which Moses saw God's promised land. When he reached the mountain, Jeremiah found a cave dwelling; he carried the tent, the Ark, and the incense-altar into it, then blocked up the entrance. Some of his companions came to mark out the way but were unable to find it. When Jeremiah learnt of this he reprimanded them. 'The place shall remain unknown,' he said, 'until God finally gathers his people together and shows mercy to them. Then the Lord will bring these things to light again, and the glory of the Lord will appear with the cloud, as it was seen both in the time of Moses, and when Solomon prayed that the shrine might be worthily consecrated.' ''

Other traditions imply that Jeremiah left Jerusalem with the Ark of the Covenant either before the Babylonian seizure of the city or sometime during the battle and secreted it in a safe place. Not everyone agrees that this mysterious hide-away is located on the mountain from which Moses first saw the Promised Land, but they all concur that it was concealed from the Babylonians and never fell into enemy hands.

For many centuries both Solomon's treasures and the legendary Ark of the Covenant were almost forgotten, remembered only when the past glory of the Israelites was discussed. But that all changed when Captain Montague Brownslow Parker set his sights for both the ark *and* the treasures and arrived in Jerusalem with only one single goal: to locate the multibillion-dollar treasure that he believed was hidden somewhere beneath the temple mount.

No one knows how the Parker expedition really began, but that the infamous operation lasted from 1909 until 1911 is now a matter of history. Rumors have it that Valter H. Juvelius, an eccentric Swedish biblical scholar and philosopher, accidentally discovered a sacred code in the book of Ezekiel while studying it in ancient manuscript form in a Constantinople library in 1908, and this code described the exact location of the long-lost treasures hidden within a tunnel system underneath the temple mount.

Juvelius teamed up with Captain Montague Parker, and, with financing of $125,000 from, among others, the Duchess of Marlborough, the Parker expedition, bribing their way through the red tape of the Ottoman Empire, worked underneath Jerusalem from 1909 to 1911, desperately searching for the elusive gold. After months of fruitless digging, tunneling, and probing, their quest came to an abrupt halt on the night of April 17, 1911, when Captain Parker and his men violated the sanctity of Islam and entered the sanctuary of the Dome of the Rock—the second most holy place in Islam. Still in the belief that the treasure was underneath the mount, their attention had been drawn to a natural cavern beneath the surface of the sacred rock. According to Jewish tradition, the place was Mount Moriah, where Abraham offered to sacrifice his son Isaac. It was also the spot from which Mohammed ascended to heaven on his horse Borek. Still other traditions held that the cavern led to the abode of evil spirits guarding an ancient treasure vault.

But Captain Parker, undaunted, felt that this was *the* night; and after lowering themselves into the cavern with ropes, his crew began to break the stones that closed off the entrance to an ancient tunnel. But, unfortunately for the expedition, one of the temple attendants had decided to spend the night on the temple mount; and, on hearing strange noises coming from the direction of the Sacred Stone, he daringly crept closer to investigate. He suddenly recoiled in utter horror when he found himself confronted with a group of peculiarly clothed foreigners, who, equally terrified upon seeing him, backed away deeper into the Holy Shrine.

Venting his fright, the attendant shrieked and ran panic stricken out of the mosque, spreading the news of the desecration of the holy place as he raced through the streets of Old Jerusalem. Within an hour the entire city was in a tumult. There was rioting in every street as rumors spread that the Englishman had discovered and stolen the Ring and Crown of Solomon, the Ark of the Covenant, and the Sword of Mohammed!

Captain Parker and his party escaped with little more than their lives and their yacht, which lay anchored in

Jaffa harbor. The political repercussions, including the replacing of the Turkish governor and the local commissioners, which followed the upheaval prevented Parker from ever returning to Jerusalem, and he never had a chance to continue his ill-conceived and badly executed venture. Ironically, proof that Valter Juvelius had actually found a secret code in the book of Ezekiel was never substantiated. It may all have been based on a hoax.

And this is where the search ended—at least until the second world war, when Marshal Rommel's army began to fall apart in North Africa. Attempting to return to Germany, small armored units broke away from his disintegrating forces and stabbed northeast, hoping to circle around Jerusalem into the Near East toward the Balkan states so as to reach the Fatherland. Fully cognizant of their plans, the Allied High Command quickly dispatched small roving armored units to the area east of Jerusalem to intercept the escapees.

A church administrator who had just returned from the Middle East in 1948 told me of the discovery made by one of those Allied armored units when we met to discuss the results of the fund-raising efforts of our group in 1947. It seemed that while one of the American units had been camping for the night somewhere in a narrow valley east of Jerusalem, it had been strafed and bombed by a German dive bomber. When one of the explosives hit the side of a cliff, it cut a hole in the rock, exposing a cave. Scrambling for shelter, several of the men clawed their way across the rubble and into the crevice.

"At first they saw nothing," he related to me; "but once their eyes had become adjusted to the dim light, they began to recognize a coffin with what looked like two angels with outstretched wings on top. It had been covered with cloth which had disintegrated and was now hanging down like torn cobwebs . . . " His story ended there, for it was all he knew or could remember. In fact, he didn't even remember the name of the man who had told it to him. It was just one of the numerous stories he had picked up while traveling through western Europe and the Middle East immediately after the war; and even though he realized it was important, he couldn't recall the details.

End of the story?

No, not quite.

Roughly twenty-five years later, an old friend hot on the trail of the Ark of Noah and the Ark of the Covenant flew halfway across the continent to my suburban Washington home with a tape recording that was nearly identical to the original 1948 report—only now many of the details that had been missing the first time were included, with the exception of the exact location. But this time a name was attached to the story, that of a U.S. Army chaplain, Captain Diefenbach, a priest who for a while in 1944 had been assigned to the 28th Field Hospital. The recording was of an interview with a former U.S. Army medic who had been with Captain Diefenbach in the same unit at the end of the war and claimed that he, Diefenbach, had told him the story.

It has been said that once you receive a serial number or a social security number you can never really get lost. Add to these the unusual name of Diefenbach and his rank of U.S. Army chaplain and the odds of locating him suddenly improve. Yet hot as the lead appeared to be, we decided to drop it for the time being in favor of pursuing the search for the "other ark"—Noah's. And it was not until 1980 that the subject of Captain Diefenbach surfaced once again. By now the search was really on, and signals were sent in all directions to find Captain Diefenbach. The Pentagon, the historical unit USAMEDS at Walter Reed Hospital, and the Catholic Military Ordinariat all became involved. The search had gone on only two weeks when our persistence was rewarded in the form of a phone call from the Ordinariat.

The mystery chaplain of the 28th Field Hospital Unit in 1944—
Captain Diefenbach. His report of having seen the Ark of the
Covenant while hiding in a cave during a bombing raid "east of
Jerusalem" sparked years of research, ending with a dead trail.
The author will appreciate any information about this man or his
wartime record.

"We do have a Captain Diefenbach on file," the spokesman told us. "He was a priest and was discharged from the U.S. Army in 1946 and assigned to the St. Theresa Church in Houston, Texas."

"Can you give us a lead as to his current address?" we inquired politely of our contact.

"Yes, certainly," was the affirmative reply. "He is with God. He died on June 10, 1959."

We had both found and lost him—all in the space of two minutes. Now the opportunity to check the various stories that had been circulating ever since 1942 ended abruptly. But the investigation could not stop as yet. The case was still too much alive.

For numerous reasons we deemed it imperative to study the captain's military records to learn the name of the unit to which he had been attached during the final phases of Field Marshal Rommel's defeat, after which it would be necessary to locate the day reports of his roving armored unit to ascertain exactly where it had been bombed and strafed. The next logical step then would be to relocate the spot by using the various coordinates listed.

It was on September 24 that we received the long-awaited telephone call from the U.S. Army Record Center in St. Louis, Missouri, the only place in the system with access to all the information needed to solve the mystery surrounding the Diefenbach story. "We hate to tell you," the impersonal voice on the other end of the line informed us apologetically, "but Diefenbach's army records were destroyed in a fire that burned eighty percent of all World War II, Korean War and World War I records. There is no way in which we can trace him or his records. As far as we are concerned, he is dead. In fact, to the Army Record Center he never even existed!"

We're still working on other leads and are slowly beginning to put back together the life of a "forgotten" man;

but since dead men tell no tales, the investigation proceeds very slowly.

Other seekers interested in the Ark of the Covenant have taken the reference in the book of Maccabees literally and have conducted searches for the ark on Mount Nebo, the mountain from where Moses first saw the Promised Land. None of these expeditions have been successful, and understandably so, for in the days of King Zedekiah, Mount Nebo was not even part of Judah, which would make it a very improbable hiding place. With so many caves within the immediate vicinity of Jerusalem, it is unlikely that Jeremiah would chance getting caught with the temple treasures and the golden ark by smuggling them through the lines of a watchful enemy, crossing the river Jordan, entering another country, and wearily scaling the jagged rocks of a mountain to finally dispose of his heavy burden.

Other approaches to the problem of locating the golden ark utilizing entirely different methods were also being developed at about the same time we were looking for Captain Diefenbach, and for the first time in history a major university was beginning to show interest in the project.

It began when Lawrence W. Blaser, a Colorado building contractor, decided to follow his dreams and turn his lifelong interest in the Ark of the Covenant into a realistic search for the fabled object. With historical records, biblical references and statements from a nineteenth-century visionary as guides, he had come to believe that the ark had to be hidden in a cave, known as David's Cave. After a visual investigation he realized that the cave he had located was far too small to have provided refuge and protection for David from the pursuing army of King Saul or to have quartered his six hundred soldiers, so he set out to discover David's real hiding place.

Having scouted the area around En-Gedi—the biblical

location of the Rocks of the Wild Goats and the Cave of David—in 1975 and 1976, he became convinced that if he could only find a large enough cave in the vicinity of En-Gedi, this would undoubtedly be David's Cave, and that within its cold and dark interior he would find the legendary Ark of the Covenant.

Blaser returned in 1977 with Frank Ruskey, a geophysical engineer, and Richard Burdick, an engineering geology technician, in order to conduct a thorough geophysical investigation for a hidden cave on the En-Gedi nature reserve. From their resistivity work and the seismic survey, combined with visual observations of the area, the scientists concluded that there was indeed a cavelike void, possibly twenty feet high, fifteen to twenty feet wide, and several hundred feet deep, with tunnels branching out like a two-pronged fork. Further visual investigation confirmed the initial impression that the cave had two possible entrances—both blocked—about ten to fifteen meters (thirty to forty-five feet) apart.

Expeditions aren't launched overnight, and it was late summer 1980 before the Blasers were able to finance a full-scale expedition to the area, under the scientific auspices of Andrew University in Berrien Springs, Michigan. It was the very first time that a scientific team had been assembled for the express purpose of finding the ark, and the seriousness of the occasion was reflected in the strategy meeting that was held in the headquarters trailer situated between the cave site and the Dead Sea, a mere eight hours before the early-morning trek to the cave. Our team was indeed a capable one, consisting of the jovial Dr. James F. Strange, an archaeologist from the University of South Florida; the bespectacled Dr. Edward Lugenbeal, a serious geoscientist from Andrews University; the lanky and soft-spoken Frank Ruskey, geophysical engineer of the U.S. Bureau of Mines; Dan Eitemiller, motion picture cameraman; and a contingent of guests and geological

View down the mountains toward the Dead Sea from the site of
En-Gedi.

The cave at En-Gedi, site of the 1979 Ark of the Covenant expedition. The rock that blocked the entrance to the cave was so enormous that only heavy equipment could have removed it.

and archaeological assistants. All that was needed now was the ark. . . .

At five the following morning the expedition members were geared up and climbing. We had studied the target through our binoculars from our campsite the day before, and the cave didn't seem all that hard to reach; but once we started our ascent, our lofty objective proved to be much more difficult to reach than anticipated. Once there, it didn't take long to clear the ground in front of the cave entrance, but instead of the mouth's being blocked by a pile of rocks stacked on top of one another as we had first thought, it was sealed off by one gigantic boulder which plugged up the entire opening. When it was time to return to camp after a day's work, all of our picks were either broken or bent. New resistivity soundings

Clearing the ground in front of the cave of En-Gedi, preparing
for the opening of the cave—that never came.

taken that day had reconfirmed the original conclusions that there was indeed a cave behind the boulder, yet we weren't any closer to getting inside than when the first pick had been raised against it that morning.

The next day, September 10, the assault continued, but to no avail. By the time we had brought in an airhammer from Jerusalem, it was clear that the job was too big for hand tools: only heavy equipment and possibly explosives could open *this* cave. Unfortunately this method had been overruled in advance by the Israeli government, since the cave was located in a wildlife reserve area. All our attempts to reach our objective had been thwarted in one way or another; and, frustrated and discouraged, we decided to pack our gear and leave the site. For the Blaser family, the investment—both financial and emotional—had been enormous, and what had taken years of preparation suddenly ended within two days without any conclusive results.

Today the blocked cave on En-Gedi Springs Hill still looks the way it did when the Blaser expedition left it on September 10, 1980. It is located only fifteen miles from the caves of Qumran where both the Dead Sea scrolls and the copper scrolls of Cave #3 were discovered. Among many of us there is still a strong feeling that the cave was blocked purposely, and that if it does not contain King Solomon's treasures, it may very well be a storage area for other artifacts.

That the search for the legendary ark is continuing was revealed in a UPI release that appeared in many U.S. newspapers during the first week of August 1981. The study had a familiar ring to it. Originating from the Durham, North Carolina, bureau, the release stated: "A team of researchers from Duke University and the University of South Florida were said Saturday to have found the first known Ark of the Covenant from ancient Palestine.

"Even though only the uppermost portion survives, this

is the first intact Ark of the Covenant that has been recovered from ancient remains," said Dr. Eric Meyers, a professor in the Duke religion department and director of the archaeological team that made the find.

"In addition to Meyers, others involved in the discovery included his wife, Dr. Carol Meyers, an assistant religion professor at Duke; and *Dr. James F. Strange, Dean of the College of Arts and Letters at the University of South Florida.*

"The ark portion discovered by the team is made of white limestone and weighs a half ton. It was found at the site of Nabratein in Upper Galilee and features two lions astride a gabled roof and a scallop shell." It was a part of an ark, but not part of *the* ark. That one still continues to elude the treasure seekers, and the search will go on until the day this revered artifact containing the tablets of stone will finally be discovered. There are those who strongly suspect that the ark is no longer in the Holy Land at all but was taken away from there many years ago. I received the first inkling of this while wandering through one of the mirrored marbled halls of the imperial palace in Addis Ababa shortly before the death of Ethiopian emperor Haile Selassi. I was impressed with the great variety and richness of the exquisitely crafted gold artifacts that adorned the walls and lined the hallways of the palace, and commented about it to my companion, General Mobratu Fisseha.

"That's because of His Majesty's ancestry," he answered proudly. "Many of his treasures are reported to date back to the very beginning of his dynasty."

"You mean . . . " I began.

"Yes," he interrupted in his own quiet way. "They date back to Ibn Hakim, or Menelik, as he is also called, the son of Makeda, the Queen of Sheba, and King Solomon."

"You're talking about a period roughly thirty centuries ago . . . "

"I know." He smiled as he watched the emperor's cheetahs, accompanied by their keeper, approach the door as they prepared for the arrival of the Lion of Judah. "But the connection is there. In fact, we call the city of Aksum the 'second Jerusalem' because of the many relics there connecting Ethiopia with ancient Israel."

And while the rest of our afternoon was spent in a meeting with the emperor, the story of the holy relics in Aksum, the ancient capital of Ethiopia and the spiritual home of the Abyssinian religion, began to take on a new dimension. And before the priests of the nearby Coptic church had finished their evening chants, I had already spent several hours reading with growing bewilderment the story of *Kebra Nagast* or "Glory of the Kings," an English translation of the fourteenth-century history of the emperor's ancestry. It was utterly unbelievable.

Its pages led me into one of the most fantastic treasure stories ever told. If we are to believe Ethiopian tradition, the Ark of the Covenant is no longer in Israel but is hidden under the ancient Church of St. Mary of Zion in Aksum, nor far from the tomb of Menelik, son of Solomon and Makeda. In *Secrets of the Lost Races* I referred to the reported ability of the ancients to travel through the skies, and in the Kebra Nagast I found a confirmation of the flight traditions I had previously discovered in the Chinese annals relating the activities of Emperor Shum (2258-2208 B.C.), who constructed his own flying machine, as well as those I had read about in the Indian classic *Mahabharata* which tells about an "aerial chariot with the sides of iron and clad with wings." The Kebra Nagast, however, ties its flight references in with the theft and the transport of the golden Ark of the Covenant from Solomon's Temple to Aksum. In Christian circles a theft of the ark by Ethiopians approximately one thousand years before Christ is totally unacceptable for a variety of reasons, all of a religious or theological nature; but the

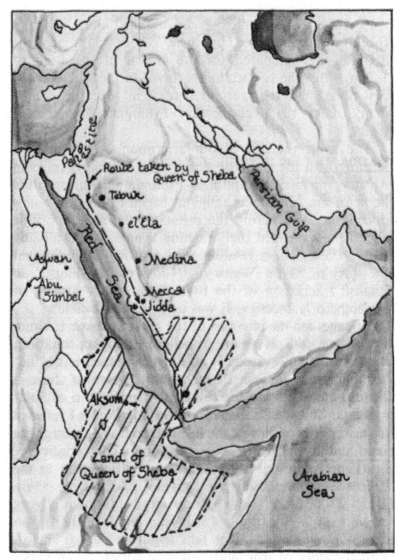

Map showing the extent of the country of the Queen of Sheba.
The arrow indicates the approximate route taken by the queen
to her capital. According to Ethiopian tradition, her son Bayna-
Lehkem stole the Holy Ark of the Covenant from Jerusalem's
temple and transported it to Aksum, where it found a resting
place under the Church of St. Mary of Zion.

unbiased investigator has to examine every story so that
an impartial evaluation can be formed.

The Kebra Nagast, a fourteenth-century compilation of
Ethiopian tradition as written by the monk Yetshak, is an
account of the kingdom of Sheba that extended across
both banks of the Red Sea. It was from this area that the
Queen of Sheba made her legendary visit to the wise King
Solomon. The biblical book of First Kings, the tenth
chapter, tells us just enough to activate our imagination:

"And when the Queen of Sheba heard of the fame of
Solomon concerning the name of the Lord, she came to
prove him with hard questions. And she came to Jerusalem with a very great train, with camels that bore spices,
and very much gold, and precious stones . . . . And King
Solomon gave unto the Queen of Sheba all her desire,
whatsoever she asked, beside that which Solomon gave
her of his royal bounty. So she turned and went to her
own country, she and her servants."

The ninth chapter of the Second Book of Chronicles
repeats basically the same account with additional details,
but the entire story has been related in only twenty-two
verses without providing any further details about the
Queen's origin, or even her race. Legends have sprung up
concerning her visit to Solomon, and many have wondered whether she really was a queen or perhaps simply a
seductress. The mystery of her visit has remained alive
throughout the centuries in legend and tradition both in
the East and the West.

But where the Bible stops the Kebra Nagast continues.
In fact, to the Ethiopians it supplies the historical basis
for the existence of the Conquering Lion of Judah. To
us it provides another lead in the search for the golden
ark.

Writing about Solomon's reaction to seeing the Queen
at his court, the Kebra Nagast reads:

"And he paid her great honour and rejoiced and he

gave her a habitation in the royal palace near him. And he
sent her food for both the evening and the morning meal
. . . and every day he arrayed her in garments which
bewitched the eyes.'' (KN,25)

"Solomon gave unto her whatsoever she wished for of
splendid things and riches and beautiful apparel . . . and
everything on which great store was set in the country of
Ethiopia, and camels and wagons six thousand in number, which were laden with beautiful things of the most
desirable kind, and wagons wherein loads were carried
over the desert . . . and a vessel wherein one could traverse the air, which Solomon had made by the wisdom
God had given unto him.'' (KN,30)

According to tradition, the Queen's meeting with King
Solomon resulted in the birth of a son called Bayna-
Lehkem nine months and five days after her return to
Sheba, and it was not until twenty-two years later that
King Solomon saw his Sheban son for the first time.
"And the youth Bayna-Lehkem was handsome, and his
whole body and his members and the bearing of his shoul-
ders resembled those of King Solomon his father, about
his eyes, and his legs, and his whole gait resembled those
of Solomon the King.'' (KN,22)

The Kebra Nagast records that soon after his arrival,
not only did Bayna-Lehkem and Solomon enter a close
father-and-son relationship, but when his newly arrived
son expressed a secret desire to take the Ark of the Covenant with him to Sheba, Solomon—according to the tradition—is supposed to have reluctantly agreed, but only if
it could be done secretly and if an exact duplicate could be
fashioned to take its place in the temple.

The actual theft of the ark is described a few chapters
later.

"And he rose up straightway, and woke up three men
his brethren, and they took the pieces of wood, and went
into the house of God—now they found all the doors

open, both that were outside and those that were inside—
to the actual place where he found Zion, the Tabernacle
of the Law of God; and it was taken away by them
forthwith . . . . And the four of them carried Zion away,
and they brought it into the house of Azarayas, and they
went back into the House of God, and they set the pieces
of wood where Zion had been, and they covered them
with the covering of Zion, and they shut the door.''
(KN,48)

The rest of the story is equally unbelievable. Claiming
that the entire caravan hovered above the ground due to
the presence of Michael the archangel, the Kebra Nagast
relates that the ark arrived at the palace of the Queen of
Sheba and eventually found a resting place in Aksum.

The story is exciting, adventurous, full of allegations
and almost unbelievable, yet what if it *was* stolen by the
Shebans, and what it if is indeed hidden away under the
Church of St. Mary of Zion in Aksum? What then about
the various accounts placing the ark still in a cave in the
Holy Land? Obviously the search which has now been
narrowed down to perhaps twenty square miles will suddenly have to include northern Ethiopia and the sacred
territory of the Coptic Church. And we will have to deal
with the furor that will erupt in religious circles if King
Solomon's treacherous act can indeed be proven. The
search for the ark may take a new turn now that Ethiopia
apparently has decided to sell some of its art treasures.
Whether their eagerness for foreign currency will go as far
as raiding their Coptic churches—thereby risking a religious uprising—will depend on the desperation of the
government. If that should be the case, the Church of St.
Mary of Zion will be a likely target, and the search for the
ark may be on again—but this time in Aksum, Ethiopia.

CHAPTER 3

Ruthless Conquerors and Barbarians with a Heart

The countries that together form the geographical area we know as the Middle East possess a charm all their own; in addition, they offer unlimited possibilities for discovery and fame to both the amateur and the professional archaeologist. In this historically rich region, the spade of the scientific inquirer has barely scratched the surface. An element of mystery permeates the area, and much of it has its origin in the stories told by early travelers and archaeologists who returned to the West accompanied by truckloads of artifacts of unknown origin—some of which predated our Western civilization by thousands of years.

Soon historians began to refer to the Middle East as the "Cradle of Civilization," truly convinced that "civilization" had the Middle East as its point of origin. In fact, until two decades ago archaeologists were even certain that agriculture was first practiced in the Middle East's fertile crescent, and that from there it eventually spread throughout the entire world. Although new excavations in various sections of the globe have proved the error of this contention, the term "Cradle of Civilization," once coined, stuck, and historians have been attempting to reinforce this somewhat hastily drawn conclusion ever since.

The treasures of the ancients come from everywhere; they are not limited to the Holy Land. Where armies battled, a host of treasure was buried; and when the tide of history turned against one empire, the victors were soon ready to move in.

Philip II of Macedon, the warrior-father of Alexander the Great, was one of those empire builders who began by forcefully uniting a severely divided Greece around the middle of the fourth century B.C. Together with his son he set out to conquer the world.

Defeating Persia was first on his list, but combining war with pleasure undoubtedly led to his destruction, for on the day his advance army of ten thousand men moved on toward the enemy, Philip decided to leave the first phase of the operation to his generals while he remained behind in Aegae for the wedding of his daughter Cleopatra to Alexander of Epirus. Scarcely had he raised the cup to his lips in a toast to the blissful pair when an assassin's dagger ended his life, leaving the scepter of power in the hands of his eager son Alexander. History has amply recorded Alexander the Great's exploits from that moment on, but gives no hint as to the exact location of his father's burial site. Considering that he was Philip of Macedon, his grave was sure to have been a rich one, even though his interment may have been conducted in secrecy.

Archaeologists may be dreamers, but they are also detectives, and the search for his tomb became an obsession for Manolis Andronicos, a young Greek archaeologist associated with the Department of Antiquities in Veroia in northern Greece. While he was still a student, his excavations in the ancient cemetery of Vergina had persuaded him that he might have stumbled on the burial plots of the Macedonian kings, and when in the fall of 1976 he dug a trench twelve meters (thirty-seven feet) deep in a large hill on the fringes of Vergina and unearthed gravestone fragments dating back to the third century

B.C., his fever mounted. Research indicated that this mound was a man-made hill hastily formed to protect and conceal the remains of Macedonian tombs from the indiscriminate hands of the grave robbers. Suddenly all his doubts were gone. Vergina could be none other than Aegae, the ancient capital of the Macedonians and the place where Philip II had been assassinated!

In August 1977 the dig continued, and all the clues seemed to coincide with this hypothesis. This was undoubtedly the royal cemetery. Could Philip's grave possibly have escaped destruction?

After more than a month of trench-digging, the outline of a small tomb came into view: but it took another three suspenseful days of excavating, measuring, surveying and photographing before attention could be focused on the marble sarcophagus that had intrigued the workers from the very first moment.

"When we lifted the covering slab, we gasped—an urn was what we anticipated," Dr. Andronicos later recalled. *"There lay a larnex, or casket, of solid gold, measuring without the legs 40 centimeters long, 33.5 wide, and 17 high. The casket and its contents weighed 10,800 grams, almost 24 pounds. The lid was embossed with a sunburst, or star with rays, while the sides were richly chased with palmettes, rosettes, and vines."* But there were more surprises waiting in the antechamber of the tomb. *"Unable to open the door,"* he continued, *"we worked like thieves again, removing a stone from the dividing wall. A second marble sarcophagus, a little larger than the one in the main chamber, stood next to the wall. An elegant golden wreath patterned in leaves and flowers of myrtle lay on the floor next to the sarcophagus."*

Not far from it lay a beautifully decorated golden quiver, while a pair of gilded bronze greaves—leg armor—were leaning almost casually against the door. Seen standing there side by side, it was obvious that they were of dif-

Sketch of the golden larnex of Philip of Macedon, father of
Alexander the Great, found by Dr. Manolis Andronicos in
Vergina, ancient burial plot of the Macedonian kings. The gold
casket measured 40 centimeters long, 33.5 wide and 17 high
and weighed almost 24 pounds.

ferent length. A quick check with a tape measure revealed that the left one was indeed a full 3.5 centimeters (1.4 inches) shorter than the right one, which measured 41.5 centimeters in length. Furthermore, it was quite obvious that there was also a difference in the shape of the shank of the left greave.

But the chamber contained still another surprise.

"Lifting the covering slab from the sarcophagus," he continued, *"we saw another golden casket, slightly smaller and simpler than the first, but with the same sunburst on the lid. Opening this priceless ossuary, we saw that the burned bones were wrapped in a rich purple fabric interlaced with threads of gold. Beside the bones lay a superb diadem of intertwined golden branches and flowers belonging to a woman. Could the bones be those of Philip's last wife, Cleopatra?"*

The entire excavation and the resulting investigation produced a collection of clues and mysteries connected by circumstantial evidence that quickened the pulse and excited the imagination. There were no inscriptions with the names of the deceased or references of a historical nature that could tie Philip of Macedonia to this specific grave, but when all the available clues were combined, an interesting picture emerged.

* It was a unique tomb in that the remains of the deceased had been placed in golden caskets—not in urns. The bones had been treated in a manner usually reserved for royalty.
* Both caskets bore the emblem of a sunburst—the royal emblem of Macedonia—on the lid.
* Among the artifacts found in the grave was a diadem: a royal headband worn only by kings and queens.
* The gilded bronze greaves—leg armor worn below the knee—that were found leaning against the wall of the tomb were of different lengths, indicating that

they had been used by a man whose gait was uneven and who had probably been wounded or maimed in battle.

* Archaeological evidence indicated that the tomb dated back to sometime between 350 and 325 B.C.

Once these hard facts were in, there was little more scientific sleuth work left to be done. Only one job remained, and that was a directed search into Macedonian history to learn the name of a maimed king who had died within that short time span.

There had only been one. He had been a cripple, and he was only forty-six years old when he died lifting a cup to his favorite daughter on her wedding day. The practiced hand of an assassin—undoubtedly hired by the victim's estranged wife Olympias—had taken his life, and Philip II of Macedonia was buried in 336 B.C. It took until 1977, 2,313 years later, to find the grave of one of history's most remarkable men.

Down through the centuries history has woven strange tales about the exploits of both Philip II and his remarkable son Alexander III, also known as Alexander the Great. But even if the legends should fade, the hoards of coins that have been found bearing the images of these conquerors will continue to keep their memory alive; and their value is enhanced by the historical significance of the hiding place and by the manner in which they were concealed.

The unexpected discovery of a collection of fifty-one golden coins of Philip and Alexander, together with a magnificent gold necklace, underneath a Hellenistic colonnade in Corinth, Greece, on March 26, 1930, is one such find. The official report of the dig written in the typically impartial style of the archaeologist, is totally devoid of all romance.

Excavator F. J. de Waele writes,

"This morning, just after breakfast, at 9:35, two workmen, digging the lowest layer just above the rock level of the Hellenistic stoa, on point P-10, find the shards of a plate which covered the groove in one quasi circular part of about 0.10 m. diameter. Inside this groove was found a hoard of 51 golden coins, of which one of them was a little toward the west in the groove. The coins are gold staters: 41 with head of Apollon and the biga; 10 with Athena with helmet of victory & AAEEAMAPOY . . . . The other important find is that of the gold necklace which was found just beside the hoard.''

While the actual value of the coins in gold amounts to thousands of dollars, their real worth is to a much greater degree determined by their origin. Numismatists, who have conducted comprehensive studies on the coins have concluded that inasmuch as the forty-one staters with the types and names of Philip II include both life-time and early posthumous issues and were coined at the mints in Pella and Amphipolis, they must have been produced prior to 333–332 B.C., since those were the only mints in proximity to Corinth. The ten staters bear clear identifying marks that assign them to the first half of the reign of Alexander, and the experts conclude that the hoard in its entirety was probably buried in approximately 329 B.C.

After having solved the questions of authenticity, origin and historical value of the treasure, we can determine with some degree of probability the circumstances that led the traitor or thief to surreptitiously bury this hoard of gold coins under the colonnade. The presence of the coins of Corinth is easily explained, for in 338 B.C. Philip had a contingent of troops stationed in the area to control the isthmus. In addition to the steady flow of money required to maintain the Macedonian outpost, history reports frequent shipments of coinage to the region. In fact, in 323 B.C. Cleander, one of Alexander's officers, had been provided with funds and sent to the Peloponnesus to enlist soldiers. Four thousand new men were added to Alexander's army during his siege of Tyre as the result of this mercenary drive. There is little doubt that the fifty-one gold coins are part of an enlistment fund that never found its way into the hands of the mercenaries but was stolen—probably by a trusted officer—and hurriedly buried in a small earthenware vessel, to lie undiscovered for twenty-three centuries.

How much gold bullion, coins and handcrafted treasures are still hidden in the caves, crevices and ruins of ancient Middle Eastern cities is a question that will never be answered fully. It may be another goatherd scouting the cliffs or another archaeologist with a dream or perhaps a youngster with a metal detector who will cause the next flurry of excitement, sending the world press scrambling to a distant place to view the newest (and possibly oldest) treasure brought to light.

But not every major discovery is made in the Middle East. In fact many important finds are now being reported from other areas rich in history but previously ignored by the West. Such is the case with a now highly celebrated discovery that had its beginning back in 1972 when Raicho Marinov, a tractor operator, pushed his mechanical blade into the rocky soil near the modern Bulgarian city of Varna on the Black Sea coast, playground of Communist commissars and well-heeled eastern European politicians and black marketeers.

While Marinov was digging a five-foot trench for an electric cable that was to connect a nearby factory to a main power line, his eyes suddenly caught the sun's reflection on a number of pieces of yellowish metal that had been exposed by the brute force of his 'dozer blade. A closer look revealed some greenish tool-like items, and a little further down in the trench some strangely shaped flake flints.

An on-the-spot investigation conducted by a hastily

called in team of archaeologists confirmed the first impression that the four-inch pieces of yellowish metal were indeed pure gold, and it was not long afterward that the initial investigators, Professor Georgi I. Georgiev of the University of Sofia and Dr. Michael Lazarov of the National Museum of Varna, turned the project over to Dr. Ivan S. Ivanov, a young archaeologist connected with the Varna Museum. It was under his direction that the trench began to yield her treasures.

The find caused great excitement in historical circles, because the obviously hammered gold had been found in the same stratum and alongside prehistoric implements clearly dating back to the Bulgarian Copper Age, which is thought to have fitted in somewhere between 5000 and 3000 B.C.: *but up to this point gold had never before been discovered in a Bulgarian Copper Age stratum.* Never before had anyone come across a Copper Age society that had adorned itself with gold!

Professor Georgiev was no stranger to the works of the unknown race of the Copper Age, for his own excavations at a settlement mound at Karanovo, 110 miles southwest of Varna, had previously brought him face to face with an assortment of artifacts and house plans that covered a time span of at least three thousand years. In fact it was there that he had discovered a 5,500-year-old clay plaque covered with strange markings which are thought to have been one of the first attempts at writing. Its real significance, however, is still undetermined, because no one has been able to find any similarity between these markings and any other known ancient inscriptions, and all attempts at translating the marks by themselves have been stymied.

Turning the new project over to the Varna Museum was like handing a man a chance to build for himself a reputation, and there is no doubt that the young archaeologist realized the importance of his assignment. Tracking down the men who had used these squares of gold became almost an obsession with Dr. Ivanov, and the trail ended where he had hoped it would: at a prehistoric cemetery dotted with graves literally filled with Copper Age gold treasure! Archaeologists who have seen the accumulation of wealth that came from the tombs have compared it to that found by Heinrich Schliemann slightly over a hundred years ago in ancient Troy. Even though in both monetary value and sheer artistic quality the Troy find far outweighs that of the prehistoric Varna graveyard, *those found at the latter location are at least 1,500 years older and are undoubtedly the world's oldest gold treasure ever found.*

It also became apparent during the excavations that even Copper Age society had its lower and upper classes, for the graves revealed that not everyone buried in Varna was interred with the same honors and overwhelming riches. Of the more than two thousand gold pieces discovered in the dirt of the graveyard, most came from four of the excavated graves, while the other disturbed gravesites appeared to be more symbolic in nature. In fact, many of them yielded nothing to indicate that anyone had actually been buried there. Instead, in several instances metal had been placed in a grave in the manner a body would have been positioned if interred. There were even graves containing clay masks to which sheet-gold features had been added. These undoubtedly had a ritualistic meaning of some sort.

While the first find caused great confusion among historians, for gold ornaments simply did not "belong" in the Copper Age, the find caused so much curiosity and unbelief that it eventually resulted in a steady flow of experts visiting the Bulgarian Black Sea coast to check the Varna site and examine the discovered objects. Dr. Colin Redfrew, professor of archaeology at the University of Southampton, England, had over a period of many years developed a theory which held that ancient people living in what is Bulgaria today had developed on their own the art and technique of melting and casting copper from ore, without relying on the technological knowledge of other civilizations. His on-the-site study now more than convinced him of the accuracy of his theory.

"At the Varna site in 1978," he wrote later on, "I found myself still in the Copper Age, but I was looking at gold, not just copper. I believe the gold was local, either panned or mined. About two thousand objects have been found in Varna, weighing in total more than twelve pounds (5.5 kilograms). My eyes popped as I beheld the golden necklaces, bracelets and breastplates, a polished stone shaft ax with gold-encased wooden handle, and a large black bowl painted in gold. When archaeologist Ivan Ivanov handed me a necklace of gold beads, I was piercingly aware that I held in my hands an object from the world's earliest gold treasure trove."

It is interesting that his theory bears a close resemblance to the one that runs like the proverbial red thread through *Secrets of the Lost Races,* a book I wrote in 1977. Many of the ooparts that have been found have made it quite obvious that our own technological development is but a rekindling of ancient knowledge attained by our "primitive" forefathers, and that the historical Flood marked the end of a highly advanced civilization and the beginning of a number of others. Noah's descendants had the arduous task of resettling the earth, but with the advantage that they could put into practice the technological breakthroughs that had been developed before the great catastrophe. Can it be that Varna was possibly located in one of those areas where Noah's descendants finally settled down?

Legend and tradition have woven a tight net of folklore around Mount Ararat in eastern Turkey, identifying it as the landing place of Noah's Ark. The Armenians in whose country the mountain is located have always referred to it as the "Mother of the World." Can there be something to this tradition?

The biblical book of Genesis, chapter 10, contains a record of the dispersion of tribes and nations in the dawning days of the Middle East which corroborates the position of the Armenian tradition. What's more, modern research fully backs the Genesis record.

Professor W. F. Albright, internationally recognized as one of the leading authorities on Middle East archaeology and history, says, "It stands absolutely alone in ancient literature, without a remote parallel even among the Greeks . . . . 'Table of Nations' remains an astonishingly accurate document . . . . (It) shows such remarkable 'modern' understanding of the ethnic and linguistic situation in the modern world, in spite of all its complexity, that scholars never fail to be impressed with the author's knowledge of the subject."

The list he refers to mentions the descendants of Noah, the offspring of his three sons. It gives the first generation of descendants of each son; what is more important, it lists their names, which often provide us with clues as to their history and dwelling place.

The first and second generations of Noah's offspring left their marks in Egypt, Palestine, Asia Minor, Assyria, Phoenicia, Armenia, the Persian Gulf region, and lands in between. The third generation moved into Europe, Spain, southern Arabia, Lower Egypt, Upper Egypt, the *Black Sea region* and Babylonia. So according to this Table of Nations, the idea of connecting the Varna craftsmen with Noah's descendants is not at all farfetched, and neither is the connection between their technical ability and pre-Flood society.

One of the reasons why archaeology has more appeal in general to amateurs and professionals than anthropology is that in archaeology the so-called missing links between ancient civilizations are continually being unearthed, making every new dig in reality a part of the total puzzle. Anthropology has been looking for the missing links between man and ape ever since Charles Darwin, and has never yet found anything that has been able to fill the gap.

A fitting example of an archaeological "missing link" surfaced in 1968 when Dr. Korium Megurtchian of the Soviet Union unearthed what is still considered to be the oldest large-scale metallurgical factory in the world, at Medzamor in Soviet Armenia. Here, 4,500 years ago, an unknown prehistoric people worked with over two hundred furnaces, producing an assortment of vases, knives, spearheads, rings, and bracelets. The Medzamor craftsmen wore mouth filters and gloves while they labored to fashion their wares of copper, lead, zinc, iron, gold, tin, manganese, and fourteen kinds of bronze. Their smelters also produced an assortment of metallic paints, ceramics, and glass. *But by far the most out-of-place discovery was several pairs of steel tweezers* taken from layers dating back before the first millennium B.C. The steel was later found to be of exceptionally high grade, and the discovery has been verified by organizations in the Soviet Union, the United States, Britain, France and Germany.

French journalist Jean Vidal, reporting in *Science et vie* of July 1969, expressed the belief that these finds point to an unknown period of high technological development. "Medzamor was founded by the wise men of earlier civilizations. They possessed knowledge they had acquired during a remote age unknown to us that deserves to be called scientific and industrial."

What makes the Medzamor metallurgical site most interesting is that it is within fifteen miles of Mount Ararat—the landing site of the survivors of the destroyed antediluvian civilizations. True, Varna is roughly two hundred miles by land and another six hundred miles by

water from Mount Ararat, or slightly farther if the entire
route is traveled by land; but Medzamor may have been
settled by the first generation after the Flood, while the
Table of Nations places the movement of people into the
Black Sea area (now northern Turkey, Bulgaria, Rumania
and Russia) during the third generation! This suddenly
places the Varna discovery in a totally different light.

But whereas the treasure of Varna was left in the
ancient burial ground by an unknown people at some
period during the Copper Age, their craftsmanship did
not die when they passed from the scene. For sake of
identification of the artifacts, archaeologists place the
stratum of the Bronze Age on top of those of the Copper
Age, followed in turn by the Iron Age and on into
recorded history. This means that others followed where
they, the Varna people, stopped. But who were "they"?
And what did they leave us as their legacy?

Treasure of the Thracians

Historical references tell us that the famed Thracians of
old lived in the land comprising the countries now known
as Greece, Bulgaria and Turkey. More important, they
arrived on the scene of history around 1000 B.C.—during
the Bronze Age. They were a barbaric people who lived
on largely uncultivated land covered with forests and
mountains filled with large mineral deposits, particularly
gold, which made the region a highly coveted possession.
It was probably their metallurgists and goldsmiths who,
having inherited their craftsmanship from the unknowns
of the Copper Age, decided to exploit the land's rich gold
deposits. They may have been the ones who first discovered the deposits of Mount Pangaion and eventually
started large-scale mining operations there. Thrace has
always been known as an area of great riches, and the
fabled mines of Pangaion were undoubtedly a major tar-

get of King Philip II of Macedonia during his conquest of Thrace in the fourth century B.C.

Evaluating both their strengths and their weaknesses, the Greek historian Herodotus arrived at his own judgment of the Thracians—one which, incidentally—is amply supported by history.

Commented he, "The Thracians are the most numerous nation in the world after the Indians, and if they were ruled by one man, or if they could agree among themselves, they would be invincible and by far the most powerful of all people . . . . But they are unable to unite, and it is impossible that they ever could, and for that reason they are weak."

Numerous and ununited? Weak and disagreeable? All true, but these are not the characteristics that we are concerned with, for thanks to the romantic science, we now recognize them also as an artistic people and lovers of treasure, and what they possessed is slowly being discovered. In fact, the richest treasure—probably the richest gold hoard ever found in one single place, with the exception of King Tut's tomb—was found in Thracian territory in 1949 near Pangyurishte, approximately ninety miles west of Karanovo. Made of the purest gold, it consisted of eight drinking vessels, and a bowl ten inches in diameter lavishly decorated with seventy-two of what appear to be African heads in relief. The workmanship showed great taste, character and style and was obviously the result of the painstaking attention of master craftsmen. Taken together, the eight vessels weighed slightly more than thirteen pounds. *Thirteen pounds of the purest gold!* Another large find was made in Vulchitrun, northwest of Karanovo. There, too, exquisite craftsmanship revealed the high artistic standards of the Thracians as well as their untold riches.

But while their arrival on the historical scene had been rather sudden, their disappearance was gradual, and in

Sometime between 375 and 350 B.C. a Thracian soldier was
buried. When his remains were unearthed, several ornaments indicative of his rank were found. One of them—a
leg guard made of gold and silver—displayed a terrifying
image of a Thracian warrior, complete with tattoo stripes
on his face, indicating his military rank.

the interim they provided the Greeks with a foundation for their music, mythology and philosophy. They eventually turned their territorial sovereignty over to a succession of conquerors. Today their country is divided among the Greeks, the Bulgarians, and the Turks. But the Thracians are not forgotten, for their barbaric way of life and their unequaled gold treasures have guaranteed them a memorable place in history. In the final analysis, it is impossible for a people to be absorbed without leaving a trace; no nation ever completely vanishes from the world scene, because the remnants of their culture remain behind as a testimony to the degree of their past greatness.

The Thracians left us their rich heritage of gold and lavishly decorated tombs which graphically depict their barbaric yet opulent way of life. But there are traces of other ancient people whose influence was even greater; their remaining tokens, however, are of a different nature from those of the Thracians. Included in these others are the Celts.

A Mysterious People with Far-Reaching Influence

No one really knows from where the Celts originally came. Even their name is somewhat of a mystery, although it is a derivative of the Greek word *keltoi,* meaning "heroes" or "lofty ones." What we do know is that they first made their appearance in central Europe during the second millennium B.C.

In the beginning they were a group of tribes unified by religion, language and culture, but it was not until the eighth century B.C.—around the time that Romulus and Remus were founding Rome and Homer was composing his *Odyssey*—that they became a dominant military and cultural force in north-central Europe, lending their language, traditions, religion and customs to the people they subjugated.

As we look back over the heritage they left us, they must have been a fantastic people. Our society owes a great deal to them. They introduced soap to the Greeks and Romans; were the first to develop seamless rims for their wheels; set our standard four foot, eight and one-half-inch railroad gauge with the span of their chariots; and brought iron to northern Europe to be used in the forging of tools and weapons. Eventually more than 150 distinct Celtic-speaking tribes, of whom the Britains and the tribes of Gaul are the most prominent, appeared in Europe to create our racial heritage.

Fascination with what the old Celts were really all about and what they might have left us as tangible evidence of their early sojourn in Europe started back in 1834 when a group of miners, digging in the old Celtic salt-mine shafts of Austria's Salzburg in the Salzkammergut region, came upon the body of an old Celt buried by a layer of salt. Surprised there by a salt avalanche which has been dated as several centuries before Christ, the two-thousand-year-old miner had literally been pickled—preserved like a salted fish. In triumph and in awe, the miners of the nearby village carried him to the church, but inasmuch as the local cemetery was the churchyard, and a heathen naturally could not qualify for a "Christian" burial, the surprise visitor was disposed of in an unknown place. But even though his remains vanished, curiosity about his origin did not. However, it was not until 1846 that the curiosity turned into action. Realizing the importance of the ancient graves in an area outside of Hallstatt, local authorities decided on a systematic excavation of the entire area. What had begun as a probe ended in a full-scale excavation resulting in the uncovering of more than two thousand graves from the Iron Age,

A variety of silver ornaments found in a Celtic grave near Szarazd-Regoly in Hungary. (Photo courtesy Hungarian National Museum)

A bronze razorback boar: a reminder to us that the Celts were extremely realistic in their art. Found in a grave near Bata, Hungary. (Photo courtesy Hungarian National Museum)

yielding enough artifacts to fill a museum. Caldrons, heavy swords, exquisitely crafted jewelry, daggers, axes and pottery brought a nearly forgotten people back to life.

But as large as the total find was, the discovery was completely overshadowed by the exhumation of a Celtic princess and her treasure near the village of Vix in eastern France in 1953, slightly over one hundred years after the first probe in the Austrian cemetery.

It was the archaeologist Rene Joffroy who was first to recognize the remains of an ancient tumulus no less than thirty-three meters (one hundred feet) across and seven meters (twenty-one feet) high, and his astute observation led to one of the most astonishing finds of the nineteenth

A Celtic silver and bronze scabbard from Kosd, Hungary. (Photo courtesy Hungarian National Museum)

century, evidence of which can now be found in the Museum of Chatillon-sur-Seine.

The Celtic princess was about thirty years old when she was buried lying atop her funerary wagon in her wood-lined grave, her head still adorned with a gold arc, the insignia of Celtic royalty. She had been laid to rest accompanied by a variety of gifts and personal belongings, including a silver bowl and amber jewelry. But the museum also proudly displays a bronze krater, lavishly decorated with Greek warriors and chariots around the very edge. In this case, it is neither the decoration nor the bronze that calls attention to the krater but rather its unusual size, for it is more than five and one-half feet in height, with a circumference of approximately thirteen feet and an overall weight of 460 pounds! Was it really made to be used? If so, the Celts must indeed have been heavy drinkers: its capacity is well over one thousand one-liter bottles.

In their enthusiasm for living, the old Celts recognized no national or tribal boundaries and could be found practically all over Europe. It may therefore be assumed that their artifacts may be found in many different locations. A casual suggestion made by a teacher from the small German village of Hochdorf to an archaeologist connected with the State Antiquities Service to "come and investigate an unusual elevated area in a nearby field" led to the eventual opening of the Celtic tomb of the Hochdorf prince, a six-foot-tall nobleman who was forty years old at the time of his death. He had rested in the field quietly amidst his most precious possessions, seemingly waiting to be called back to life. Yet here too it was not only the prince but also that which surrounded him in death that made his tomb one of the most exciting Celtic graves of the century.

Jorge Biel, the state archaeologist in charge of the excavation, could barely conceal his pride about the discovery and remain scientifically sober and impartial when he penned his recollections of seeing the Hochdorf prince for the very first time. "The prince's skeleton lay on the three-meter-long sheet of bronze, actually a funeral bed," he wrote later on. "Gold jewelry was strewn over the remains and in fragments of his clothing, which had been made from richly patterned cloth with embroidery in Chinese silk.

"The Hochdorf prince wore an important status symbol of a Celtic chieftain of the Hallstatt period—a necklace in the form of a gold ring," he continued. "His clothing was fastened with intricately twisted gold brooches. A delicate band of gold adorned his wide leather belt. The hilt of the noble's dagger had been plated with gold, and he wore a wide gold armband. Thin strips of gold had embellished the prince's shoes—a novelty in the field of Celtic archaeology.''

But that wasn't all, for this tomb too contained much more than just a skeleton adorned with an assortment of gold ornaments. The greatest surprise was the bronze bier

One of the eight cast-metal statues of women that supported the funeral bed of the Hochdorf prince. "Those figures balance, almost like circus acrobats, on functional wheels of bronze and iron; the whole affair could be rolled like a sofa on casters." (Photo courtesy Dr. J. Biel)

which had been used as a final resting place for the prince. "In the form of a high-backed bench," Biel reported, "the great bed was supported by eight cast-metal statues of women a foot high. These figures balance, almost like circus acrobats, on functional wheels of bronze and iron; the whole affair could be rolled like a sofa on casters." Nothing like this had ever been found before. The Bronze Age just wasn't supposed to have been that sophisticated!

That the prince's family had taken great care to assure his well-being in the hereafter showed clearly in the many provisions they had made for him. A huge four-hundred-liter bronze caldron still contained the dried remnants of the mead with which they had filled it at the time of the funeral, and bronze platters and plates as well as an assortment of slaughtering and carving tools were stacked on a four-wheeled serving cart across the tomb.

By now, many Northern, Western and even American art collectors are slowly expanding their private hoards of illegally acquired artifacts retrieved from the raided tombs of ancient nations. About those artifacts—many of which are rumored to be gold—specific details are difficult to obtain and the locations of the illegal collections even harder to trace. But with both the Thracians and the Celts, it is as if the pressure of time is now forcing them into the front of history, drawing archaeologists as if by magic to their unmarked graves, calling them to the rescue.

Lifting the Veil of Secrecy

The secrecy which has become the way of life in the Soviet Union has also put its censorship stamp on the inoffensive but imaginative science of archaeology. But, once discovered, treasures are almost impossible to keep hidden, no matter how much "decadence" they represent, for the exchange of scientists and their published reports in scholarly journals often supply sufficient leads about new discoveries to initiate serious probes—often with startling results.

I vividly remember sitting on the terrace of the Nile Hilton in Cairo a number of years ago, comparing notes on a recent news development in the Middle East with a competing journalist from the Russian news bureau Tass. During the course of our conversation the Russian dropped a hint about startling archaeological discoveries being made in the Soviet Union. When I pressed him for details, he ducked. "Just take my word for it," was his irritated answer. "Tombs, artifacts, remnants of old civilizations, and real treasure have been found . . . ."

I pointed into the direction of the pyramids. "Anything comparable to what came from there?" I queried.

He remained noncommittal. "Someday you'll hear about it."

It was not until several years later that, while combing through some partially translated Russian archaeological reports, I began to realize what he had been hinting at. Russia and the various people's republics that together form the USSR have always been somewhat of a mystery to the West. The discoveries that have been made in those countries have only added to the intrigue instead of lifting the veil, but even the little bits of information that have leaked out have inadvertently caused steadily increasing curiosity among collectors of rare art and dealers in archaeological artifacts.

In Issik in Kazakhstan, not far from Alma Ata, a dig which started more or less as a routine excavation turned into a major find for the Russians when it led to the discovery of a body dating back to the fifth century B.C., lavishly surrounded by more than a thousand gold objects. The gold added glamour to the somber gravesite, and even though the origin of the ornate gold objects is uncertain (it has been suggested that they may have been left behind by passing caravans in the form of a tribute or taxes), the real mystery of the grave was a finely hand-crafted silver vase. Engraved with twenty-six signs or characters, it appears to tell a story—but of what or about whom no one is certain. One thing is sure: the inscription bears a very close resemblance to early Scandinavian and Anglo-Saxon writing, which may indicate that there was a possible trade connection between Kazakhstan and western Europe as far back as 500 B.C. Where are the objects now? The Russians aren't saying.

Slightly more has become known about the treasure retrieved from the small mound of Tillya-Tepe (Golden Hill), located a mere three miles (five kilometers) northwest of the city of Shibergan in northwestern Afghanistan, an area that was formerly part of the empire of the Great Kushans. The results of the work of the expedition did not receive the worldwide acclaim and international press coverage accorded Howard Carter's opening of King Tut's tomb, yet now the find is said to rival that one in overall richness.

Like so many significant discoveries, this one had an innocent beginning, a casual probe into a small, seemingly unimportant mound of dirt back in 1969. It was not until two years later that careful digging indicated that the site dated to the end of the second or the beginning of the first millennium before Christ. But even then, expectation was low; no one anticipated a major find. Tillya-Tepe was left unattended and at the mercy of the elements until 1977, when a joint Afghan-Soviet expedition led by the renowned Russian archaeologist Victor I. Sarianidi followed up on the findings of the preliminary probe and turned it into a full-scale excavation.

The digging, scraping and brushing that followed soon revealed the remains of a monumental structure that had been erected in antiquity on a block platform about nineteen feet (six meters) in height that had been enclosed by a fortification which stood more than thirty feet (ten meters) high. In the interior, remains of columns and even parts of an ancient altar were discovered, giving credence to the growing impression that Tillya-Tepe was the site of an ancient fire temple—in itself a major discovery. Under the guidance of the professionals, local tribesmen continued digging and soon not only cleared the temple structure but began working on the slope of the hill as well. It was there that several burial vaults were discovered, leading the way to human remains and a cache of jewelry that included gold objects weighing up to one kilogram (two pounds) apiece.

"We have every reason to believe that the graves discovered at Tillya-Tepe belonged to the local aristocracy, possibly the royal family of the Great Kushans who resided at Yemshi-Tepe," reported Dr. Sarianidi upon his discovery. "Moreover, the discrepancy between the rich funeral offerings and the modest, almost primitive grave construction could indicate that interment took place secretly, most likely at night." Of the seven graves found, six were excavated. The richness of the find was evident from the start, for while the caskets had been entombed without lids, cloths sewn with silver or gold disks covered them, and in one instance grape leaves were used as ornaments on the cloth.

There is no complete list available showing the exact number of items together with detailed descriptions of the Kushan treasure, but a sketchy inventory compiled from the various reports reveals that it included among others:

* Two burial crowns with gold pendants and pearls.
* Massive gold plates cast in the shape of five-petaled rosettes, with turquoise inlays.
* Gold figured plates, inlaid with worked stones such as turquoise, carnelian and garnets.

* Gold multi-petaled roses.
* Necklaces consisting of hollowed beads.
* A cast gold hoop with open end weighing 850 grams (almost two pounds), found on the neck of one of the deceased.
* Gold clasps to hold the richly ornamented garments together.
* Two gold scabbards. On one, a chain of beasts following one another is presented in high relief. The claws and sharp-toothed jaws of each animal tear into the hindquarters of the preceding creature. A winged griffin grabs the leg of the dragon in front of it; the dragon, in turn, with jaws opened wide, makes an attempt to bite the leg of the next winged beast. It is obvious, however, that the artist who fashioned the scabbard was not without humor. Considering the ongoing struggle between the animals, one would expect a dramatic climax at the top of the handle. But it ends peacefully, with a figure of a bear cub, leaning restfully on its hind legs, good-naturedly nibbling on a bunch of grapes . . . .

The cloak of secrecy is slowly being lifted from the Kushans. It is not that they tried to hide from us; history has simply covered them up. To the West they are still little more than a name, and most history books don't even mention them. Barely mentioned by the Greco-Roman authors, they fit in "somewhere" within the dark ages of the history of the area, a lost race of forgotten people.

Scythians—Men of Cruelty and Wealth

Say the words "Africa" and "wealth" and one immediately thinks of South African gold mines, the fabulous treasures of the Queen of Sheba, or the riches of Emperor Haile Selassi. When wealth is spoken of in connection with Russia, the treasures of the Imperial Russian household come to mind. While still a small boy, I used to listen to stories about the Russian crown prince Peter going to the Netherlands to study shipbuilding. In later years I interviewed one of the escaped palace guards of Tsar Nicolas on the Dutch island of Terschelling and listened to his recollections of the Russian revolution of 1917 and the plundering hordes of revolutionaries who stole or smashed the imperial treasures displayed throughout the palaces. But destructive as they were, the mobs that ransacked the buildings and massacred the family of the tsar could not erase the indelible marks that history had made upon the country. Those marks were there to stay, left there to be rediscovered—first by the grave robbers of the eighteenth century, and later by scientists in search of history.

Some of the republics belonging to the USSR have a vicious past, and the Ukraine is among them. It was to this area that the nomadic tribes from the region of the Altay Mountains on the border of China migrated in the eighth century. Known under the collective name of the Scythians, these thundering, beastly warriors soon established for themselves a notoriety that has echoed throughout the centuries. Their reputation for cruelty far surpassed that of any other race, but tangible evidence even of their existence remained elusive for many centuries. Only the descriptions of them left us by the fifth-century Greek writer Herodotus of Halicarnassus, the "father of history," kept the memory of their exploits alive—for the horror story given by Herodotus when he describes the Scythians is a nightmare come to life.

In his fourth book of history, produced as a result of his visit to Olbia, a Greek city founded around 645 B.C. at the confluence of the Bug and Ingul rivers, Herodotus describes the Scythians as fierce warriors who beheaded their enemies, sometimes making coats, capes and cushions out of their skins. They were men who rarely bathed, who drank the blood of those they conquered, and who often saved the top part of their victims' skulls to be used as drinking vessels after covering the outside with cowhide and gilding the interior with gold. Their frenzied behavior when going into battle has become legendary, as has their liking for strong, undiluted wine and the smoking of hashish . . . .

Nevertheless, they were stunning military strategists and exquisite craftsmen. Although religious in their own way, they did not settle anywhere long enough to erect temples to their gods. They were always on the move, wedded to the steppes. Commented Herodotus: "Having neither cities nor forts, and carrying their dwellings wherever they go; accustomed, moreover, one and all, to shoot from horseback; and living not by crops but from their cattle, their wagons the only houses they possess, how can they fail of being unconquerable and unassailable?"

All we really knew of them we gleaned from his references, and from the fact that Scythian power and brutality remained intact until the fourth century B.C., when they had to give way to the Sarmatian invaders and were eventually destroyed as a powerful force sometime during the second century A.D. It was as if an impenetrable pall of silence had been cast over the Scythians; as if history had conspired to suppress them forever because of their insane cruelty. Only the Greek historian had been allowed to tamper with history's judgment.

The spell was finally broken when a Siberian gold-mine owner sent a gift to Peter the Great, tsar of all the Russias, in 1715. The surprise gift, consisting of twenty pieces of exquisite gold art, greatly aroused the curiosity of Tsar Peter. When shortly thereafter news of other discoveries reached him, he realized the importance of these historical artworks and ordered all looting and grave robbing stopped and all the known gravesites protected. For many

The influence of Greek craftsmen can be found in virtually
every piece of Scythian art. This segment of a gold breastplate
depicts men sewing the skin of a lamb or sheep to form a tunic.
(Museum of Historical Treasures, Kiev, USSR)

of them the protective measures had come too late; and,
in fact, his order had little or no effect, since grave robbing did continue, even picking up in intensity after the
death of the tsar in 1725.

As a result of the work of the grave robbers and scientific persistence, Herodotus' account has been amply supported by the additional knowledge that has come our
way through the methodical opening of the Scythian
kurgans, or funeral barrows, which rise like hills from the
Russian steppes. Some of them are more than one hundred yards across at the base and measure nearly sixty feet

This two-inch gold plaque, a fine example of Scythian art, dates back to the fourth century B.C. It is on display in the State Hermitage Museum in Leningrad, USSR.

high—and all to protect the bones, relics and personal belongings of the Scythian chieftains or kings. Russia's museums can now boast of a near-unbelievable collection of gold artifacts, a dazzling array of exquisitely formed creations that betray the Scythians' sensitivity for detail and love of animals and reveal the importance gold had in their brutal society. When Herodotus wrote that the Scythians were "immensely rich," he unknowingly penned the understatement of the century.

How rich this Scythian treasure really was can be judged by looking at some of their ornaments now proudly displayed in museums such as the State Hermitage Museum in Leningrad and the Museum of Historical Treasures in Kiev. During excavations in Kostromskaya Stanitsa, a gold stag plaque, probably the central ornament from a shield, dating back to the sixth century B.C. was found. The plate depicts a stag in reclining position with its head arched. Other stags almost as beautiful as the one displayed in Leningrad have been found in Hungary and the Crimea. Other solid-gold ornaments uncovered include a gold comb with a molded group of highly realistic figures showing a battle between Scythians. Because the horseman on the comb is wearing a Greek helmet, the opinion has been offered that the artist probably was a Greek in service of the Scythians. The influence of the Greeks on Scythian art is also embodied in another fine piece of gold art on display today in the Museum of Historical Treasures in Kiev. It is the central part of a breastplate, depicting two Scythians sewing an animal skin to make a tunic or jacket. Also displayed is the end piece of a collar made of twisted metal, known as a torque, showing the delicately modeled figure of a bareback horseman. The Scythians were famous for their torques, and many of them have been recovered from kurgans throughout former Scythian territory.

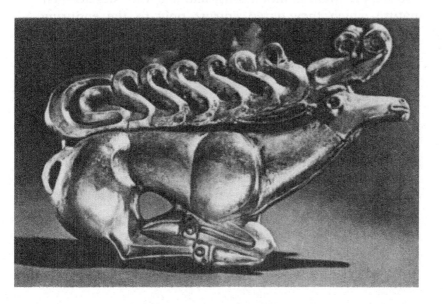

One of the Scythian burial mounds at Kostromskaya in the
Caucasus surrendered this beautifully handcrafted plaque of a
stag in reclining position. The stag was a favorite animal among
the peoples of the steppes, and many plaques like this one
have been found throughout the area occupied by the
Scythians. This one dates back to approximately 700 B.C. and
is in the collection of the State Hermitage Museum in Leningrad,
USSR.

The vast collections of solid-gold Scythian art pieces
now held by major Russian museums and by private art
collectors are worth literally hundreds of millions of dollars for their gold value alone, not to mention their value
as pieces of art; but the question of how so brutal and
barbarous a nation as the Scythians could show so much

artistic feeling has thus far remained unanswered. Perhaps these barbarous men, who as maniacal nomads ruled the steppes and the mountains, had a gentler side to their nature which they dared entrust only to the enduring beauty of gold.

CHAPTER 4

An American Enigma

The month was April. The year was 1981. And the flight was Delta #10, bound for London, England. This should have been a happy occasion for me, for I had grown weary of the spring rain that had fallen for days on end; and according to the weather reports London was surprisingly balmy. Yet somehow I had an uneasy feeling that this trip wouldn't turn out as expected. Call it a hunch. At that moment, however, I was too tired and sodden to care.

Only after I had positioned myself in my window seat did I open my black Samsonite attaché case—I needed one last look just to assure myself that the woolly red pouch with the metal pot was still inside. Then—before anyone else could cast a curious glance at its contents—I hurriedly closed the case, turned the dial of the combination lock, and pushed it under the seat in front of me.

It was a strange set of circumstances that had put me on that plane, and the mysterious pot was responsible. It had all begun—as so many stories do—with a simple telephone call. I had just reached my office from a research job at the library when the phone rang. A reader of one of my most recent books, *Secrets of the Lost Races,* had

become fascinated with the subject of out-of-place artifacts as discussed in the book, and the references I had
made to the possibility of this country's having been visited by representatives of other races thousands of years
ago. "You talked about those 'ooparts'—those out-of-
place artifacts," the caller pointed out, "and I think I
know just what you were talking about. I have something
which clearly does not belong in the area where it was
found. Would you like to see it?"

The question was innocent enough, but it started a
series of long telephone conversations that finally resulted
in the caller, John Van Asselberg, a semi-retired farmer,
offering to bring his oopart to my office within the next
few weeks.

When John finally arrived after his six-hundred-mile
ride on a Greyhound bus and we had checked him into a
motel in Chattanooga, he proudly pulled a carefully
wrapped package out of the shopping bag he had been
carrying. Opening a soft woolly pouch that obviously had
been made especially for the pot, he carefully reached
inside and almost reverently took out his oopart. "This is
what I called you about," he said softly with a tremble of
excitement in his voice. "What do you think of it?"

Before me on the faded blue bedspread stood a yellowish metal vase about four and a half inches high and
about seven inches in diameter. I had traveled widely and
had visited dozens of museums the world over to examine
archaeological artifacts, but this vessel was unlike anything I had ever seen. It had the deep yellow hue of gold,
yet when I touched and tapped it, it had the hardness of
copper. I picked it up and walked over to the window to
examine it more closely by daylight. Turning it slowly so
as to get a better overall view of the elaborate artwork, I
was overwhelmed by the feeling that it seemed to tell a
story of some sort—a detailed version of a happening in
the far-distant past.

John came closer and began to describe it as if it were a member of his immediate family. By now he had lived with the pot for so long and had attempted to interpret the meaning of the hammered figures so many times that he could talk about the particulars of each one without even looking at them. It was under his guidance that for the first time I began to notice the little special details about each one of the figures.

The pot is an object that cannot stand in a room without becoming the center of attention. It has a mystical quality that begs for attention, as though it carries a special message awaiting revelation.

The people whose forms are etched into the pot are of three distinctly different types; the most oustanding figure is a tall white-bearded man who is without a doubt the central character in the pot's story. Aside from him there are nine smaller human beings depicted in headdress, and another thirteen with a totally different hairdo. Positioned to the left of the bearded man is a large image of the sun-god. Both the sun-god and the old man display what appear to be tufts of hair on their foreheads. This fixture is also visible on the heads of some of the smaller people.

The facial features of the humans are all very similar, displaying almost almond shaped eyes and Semitic noses. Located exactly opposite the sun-god on the other side are two large sphinxes and a much smaller one; none of the three is typically Egyptian in appearance. The section of the vase opposite the old man is taken over by two realistically crafted large fish, scales and all; so large that they, together with the old man, the sphinxes and the sun-god, form the main themes of the story of the pot. But between these central figures every bit of metal is covered with designs such as groupings of three pyramids; a tree or tree branch; elephants, birds, and other animals. And where no distinctly recognizable figures have been hammered

The mysterious-looking gold-colored pot that was discovered in an old cave or root cellar 45 miles east of Kansas City, Missouri, in 1959. An analysis of slivers of metal taken from the pot indicates that it consists of copper, zinc, lead, iron, and a trace of tin. This puts it in a class of ancient brass that has not been used for more than a thousand years. Notice the figure of the bearded man in the right foreground.

This side of the copper pot shows one of the two fish that form a major design element.

Another view is a representation of the sun-god, surrounded by
a court of attendants. The small human figures appear to pay
homage to the two central (God) figures on the pot.

On this side of the pot, attendants in various poses surround
two sphinxes who seem to be eyeing each other. The style of
the sphinxes lead us into the direction of the Middle East—not
Latin America.

into the metal, the formerly smooth spaces have been filled up with triangular marks resembling cuneiform writing.

"What do you make of it?" John asked hesitantly. "Can it be an oopart?" I handed the vase back to him and sat down on a corner of the bed. "Tell me the whole story, John. Tell me where you got it, where it came from, who had it before you . . . . Let's go over the whole story so I can try to make some sense out of it, for if it is indeed an oopart and it was found in the United States . . . " I stopped. I didn't want to run ahead on any possible conclusion, for whatever John Van Asselberg had to tell about it would certainly have to be checked out before any conclusion could be reached.

Later on that same evening we sat down in my office, where John recalled his developing involvement with the pot.

"For me it began sometime between August 16 and 30 back in 1975," he slowly began. "We had gone to Missouri and bought a truckload of used furniture and collectable junk from Frank Lee, a friend of mine in Warrensburg. I bought the load for resale, but while going through Frank's stuff I noticed that little pot he had on a shelf, and seeing that we were interested in it, he gave it to me. He didn't see any value in it. So we took it home. But it was not until we cleaned it in February of '76, along with a bunch of other metal articles we had picked up, that my wife suddenly noticed the beautiful designs under the muck. Up to that point it had been covered with about a quarter of an inch of a thick, heavy tarlike substance, but when the solvent began to cut through it, Betty became all excited. Sensing that we had found something unusual, we began to show it to antique dealers and auctioneers, hoping to find out something about its origin and how much it could be worth; but everyone we asked about it referred us to someone else. We decided to go a step higher and began to ask people in colleges and universities, until we ended up at the office of Dr. Paul R. Cheesman of Brigham Young University in Provo, Utah, where we got our first positive results. Metal analysis conducted by a colleague of Dr. Cheesman revealed that its composition of copper, zinc, lead, iron and a trace of tin classified it as an ancient brass that had not been produced for more than a thousand years.''

According to the Van Asselberg account, the metal analysis sent Dr. Cheesman's curiosity into high gear; and their second meeting, scheduled for two days later, was postponed for six days to enable Dr. Cheesman to fly to Harvard University to consult with Dr. Barry Fell, president of the Epigraphic Society and a master in the deciphering of ancient inscriptions.

"We waited in our Provo motel for a whole week," said John Van Asselberg somewhat disgustedly, "and when he finally came back, he was reluctant to give the pot back to us. We pressed him to tell us some of the results of his meeting with Dr. Fell, and he finally admitted that various factors—including the metal analysis—had led them to believe that it was from a thousand to fifteen hundred years old, possibly even older, but that it was definitely Christian . . . . They believe the tall bearded man to be Christ and the sun-god to denote that the man is the Son of God. Since that time Dr. Fell has taken the pictures and slides of the pot to North Africa and consulted with other archaeologists, and they have determined that it is not from their area. Dr. Cheesman has checked with experts from South America, and it isn't from their part of the world either. Dr. Fell is supposed to have said that it could be from North America . . . ''

Perhaps it was time for me to have a talk with Frank Smith, the man who had sold the pot to John Van Asselberg in the first place, to see how far we could go in tracing it back into history.

Frank was home and willing to talk. "I didn't buy it or
get it from anyone, and I really don't know who owned it
before me. I moved out here in 1959, and about thirty or
forty yards from where I built my house in '63 were the
remains of an old foundation. I was told there used to be
an old log cabin in that spot. We were clearing out the cellar when we came upon the pot in the rubble. It was
mixed with sand and all sorts of junk, and we had to dig it
out.

How deep was the foundation hole?

"Oh . . . it was just about three or four feet deep in
the red sandstone and about eight or nine feet around. We
wanted to fill in the hole and decided to clear it out first.
We hauled all the other stuff off and threw it away, but
when we found this old pot we decided to save it. Looked
like something we could use. We did some cleaning, put a
little chain on it, and even had some flowers in it at one
time. Later on it ended up in our basement.

"Guess we must have kept it there for about ten years or
so. Had a lot of people come and look at it. It was a fascinating conversation piece. We sold things from the basement, and I'd always say, 'Hey, you've got to see this.
We've got something interesting here!' and they'd come
and look at the little 'grabber' and it would really puzzle
them . . . especially the old man and the fish . . . "

" 'Little grabber?' What do you mean, 'little
grabber?' "

He laughed. "We called it our 'little grabber' because it
would get their attention. They all looked at it and stared
at it, but of course no one knew what the thing was all
about. When I think back on it now, it probably tells a
story of some kind . . . "

"What did the pot look like when you dug it up?"

Frank was quiet for a moment, letting his thoughts drift
back to 1959, now twenty-three years ago, and the cool
breezy fall morning on his eighty acres forty-five miles
east of Kansas City, Missouri.

"It was real dirty, and the black stuff stuck to it like glue,"
he remembered. "I guess it was the shape more than anything else that made us keep it, because it really didn't look
like much when we happened on it. I have always wondered
where it came from. What makes the pot especially interesting to me is the area where we found it. About seven hundred
feet from the cave is the old Hussy Springs that has been
there for centuries—as long as people have been here, I
guess, and probably even longer. It used to be a watering hole
for caravans and travelers and Indians and later on for the
cavalry during the Civil War. It has such a good supply of
water that the government put a gasoline pump on it during
the early thirties so the whole neighborhood could get water
from the Ol' Hussy . . . . It has always been there for whoever passed by.

"Another point of interest in the area is a mysterious
mound of dirt on my neighbor's property, northwest of
Hussy Springs. It is a hill—four to six feet high and about
ninety to one hundred feet in diameter—and no one really
knows what it is."

He stopped and laughed. "Do you think that old pot
really means something?"

His question brought us right back to square one: the
mystery of the Van Asselberg pot. Thinking about the territory where it was found and the history of the Ol'
Hussy, I began to daydream about ancient scouting parties from faraway lands venturing inland into unknown
territory, perhaps burying their chieftains in mounds of
dirt which are still undisturbed.

The idea of the American continent's having been visited by ancient races thousands of years before Columbus
is not new anymore. In fact, it is gaining more ground
every day, but it may take a new and more imaginative
brand of scientist to recognize the data that will prove the
theory correct. Many inscriptions now being found
throughout the United States are judged to be thousands
of years old.

In another book I discussed the idea that the Chinese were among the first to visit the North American continent—basing it on the *Shan Hai King, the Classic of Mountains and Seas,* a treatise on geography and one of the oldest surviving Chinese literary works. The date for its composition has been approximated at 2250 B.C., and its authorship has been ascribed to the "Great Yu." His descriptions of the geographical features of certain sections of the United States are so precise that it becomes very evident from the accuracy of his details and personal observations that the Chinese indeed made an extensive survey of the North American continent some forty-five hundred years ago!

Proof of their presence in America has also been found in the form of rock script in various places. In British Columbia, petroglyph expert Philip Thornburg recognized among the stone pictures a carving of a *sisuti*—the Chinese dragon. Says Thornburg, "There does seem to be an oriental background to them. Since they are carved in sandstone, it is virtually impossible to say what age they are. I have found some that were buried under a foot of topsoil. Now this wasn't the kind of topsoil that would have washed over them. *This was formed there,* placing the age of the carving around five to seven thousand years—which is really ancient for this country." Another petroglyph he discovered had a hole worn through it by dripping water, proof that it had been there for some time.

Among those who believe that America was once visited by ancient races who left stone inscriptions as their "calling cards," Dr. Cheesman and Dr. Barry Fell stand out above all others because of their deep devotion to study in this area.

Dr. Fell strongly believes that America was never really isolated. It is his conviction that ancient people came here for the same reasons modern immigrants do—to get away from the pressing problems at home, whether they be taxation, tyranny or marital difficulties. "We know this from inscriptions occurring on buried temples, on tablets, on gravestones and on cliff faces," he points out. "From some of them, we infer that colonists intermarried with American Indians, so their descendants still live here today." The earliest arrivals, he believes, came here around 900 B.C., and he uses inscriptions on boundary markers bearing family names as proof for his position.

Gloria Farley of Heavener, Oklahoma, a determined amateur archaeologist, is responsible for discovering many of the inscriptions left in this country by some of the early travelers. Climbing rugged bluffs and crawling into slime-covered caves to discover her finds, she then submits them to Dr. Fell for translation. One of her most remarkable discoveries is an inscription containing letter and pictograph carvings of human figures found along a quarter of a mile of cliff in the Cimarron region between Colorado and Oklahoma. One set of letters reads: "Edict: Mara's settlement. Let it be known." A figure of a female with lettering beneath her knees was identified by Dr. Fell as the Phoenician goddess Tanit, wife of Baal. The lettering reads: "Tanit the Sublime," and he calls it "the first clearly labeled representation of a Mediterranean divinity in the Americas."

Gloria Farley has her own theory as to how the ancients reached the Southwest and other regions of the American continent. "The answer," according to Mrs. Farley, "is on any good map." She claims that since the rivers of the region of the Southwest—the Arkansas, the Cimarron— are all connected to the Mississippi, the visitors had only to navigate their graceful ships up this great waterway and move out from there. Interestingly, she has discovered a carving of an ancient ship on a panel of stone beside a Cimarron River tributary about three miles' distance from where the carving of the goddess Tanit was found. Is it possible that the three pyramids and the three sphinxes on the Van Asselberg pot are pointing toward a Middle East origin?

The puzzle of the pot's origin has led scientists to several archaeological "hotbeds"—but all have been dead ends. The pyramids and the sphinxes lead us toward a Mediterranean point of view; the pyramids and the sungod seem to indicate a South American connection. The possibility of its having originally come from Latin America appears to have been uppermost in the mind of Dr. Cheesman when he saw the artifacts for the first time. He admitted that he recognized a similarity between it and the Crespi collection—a collection of possibly pre-Flood origin housed in a small museum in the back patio of the Church of Maria Auxiliadora at Cuenca in Ecuador. Yet a closer examination of the pot also emphasizes some of the striking *dis*similarities between it and the pre-Inca art.

Comments Jack Vivison of Leesville, Louisiana, "One does not have to be an expert art critic to catch the general mood of the 'common mortals' in the background [referring to the pot]. They are undoubtedly paying homage to these two gods in the most humble way they could possibly present themselves. Those between the two gods have their hands over their hearts, while others stand with arms folded. This is what is called 'picture writing,' and was of course used by ancient peoples before the introduction of hieroglyphics. It is quite possible that each individual represents other information that we are not aware of by expression of body and limb positions, attitude and position of head, facial expression, manner of dress, headbands, and perhaps even the length of their noses. It would certainly be fascinating if one could read each detail.''

The pot has remained much of a mystery since its discovery nineteen years ago. Dr. Cheesman's opinion has brought us no closer to an acceptable answer, nor did those of the experts of the various antiquities departments of the British Museum who examined it with a great deal of curiosity when I arrived.

The latter experts finally came up with their definitive answer.

"It does not belong in our department," a spokesman for the department of Middle Eastern archaeology told me, handing the red pouch and pot back to me. "We have nothing in our department which we can use as a basis for comparison . . . ."

"Can you make any suggestions?"

"Not really. Although I suppose you could talk to people in Greek and Roman archaeology . . . " So I did.

Walking through the marble exhibit halls of the British Museum with a yellow-gold object that had all the earmarks of belonging somewhere behind glass did occasion the uninvited attention of some of the guards, but it all ceased once I was safely within the confines of the research department of Greek and Roman antiquities. Their experts too looked at it—and shrugged their collective shoulders. "Wish we could help you," was the final verdict, "but we can't identify it. May we suggest you try the department of Middle East archaeology? You could also try Indian art or African art, or some other department or . . . " The attendant was still mumbling as I walked down the marble steps on the way to my favorite Greek restaurant for some shish kebab and a piece of baklava before heading for Gatwick airport and the Delta Airlines ticket counter.

While in London I had checked all of the possible leads that I thought promising in identifying the artifact, and none of them had brought me any closer. But in the rush of it all, I had skipped one. It wasn't until a year and a half later that the Victoria and Albert Museum supplied a piece of the puzzle.

"In my opinion, the bowl is probably from the Daghestan area of the Caucasus," wrote an archaeologist of the department of metalwork in a letter dated October 29, 1981, "and is almost certainly from the nineteenth century." It was *some* help—at least as far as a possible location was concerned. As for the dating, all the museum had seen for identification purposes was a number of black and white photographs—not the results of the metal analysis, or the pot itself. Their identification was based on the shape of the vessel and some of the artwork which had become somewhat traditional in that specific area. So while it did not help in setting the time period, it was a help in finding its possible point of origin.

But we are still a long way from answering all the questions that have been raised by the discovery of the Van Asselberg pot. For instance:

How did a copper pot, fashioned less than two hundred miles from Mount Ararat, the "Mother of Nations," end up in a red sandstone cave forty-five miles southeast of Kansas City, Missouri, in close proximity to an ancient watering hole?

Does its presence in Missouri have anything to do with the undisturbed mound nearby?

Are there other, similar, vessels in the United States that might help in further identifying the pot?

Is it possible that there are more objects, left by the same people, still buried somewhere in the Middle West?

Did the pot have any religious significance for its original owners? Was it brought here for a specific purpose?

Who is the old man on the pot? Who is represented by the disk of the sun? What do the three pyramids signify? How about the fish? And, above all, what is the story that has been so carefully hammered into the brass? What is it trying to tell us?

CHAPTER 5

China's All-Seeing Eyes

"Every man an archaeologist and every woman a historian" is a slogan almost as catchy as the one found prominently displayed in most American union halls: "A Good Woman Is a Union Woman." Not everyone in the U.S. agrees with the latter; but just about everyone in Communist China happily attempts to live up to the first one. Recovering the triumphs of the past is beginning to be extremely important to the government of the People's Republic of China.

When Chiang Kai-shek's government fled mainland China in 1949 and strengthened their hold on the island of Formosa, renaming it Nationalist China, they did not go empty-handed. They took with them an enormous collection of archaeological artifacts and Chinese historical treasure. So complete was their "stripped earth" policy that when their withdrawal had been completed and the Nationalists had regrouped on Taiwan, it was as if China had completely lost its historical heritage. There was very little left that could be used by the incoming Mao Tsetung regime on which to base its continuity of government. Furthermore, as a country with a colorful history that dates back for thousands of years, the Chinese people have always possessed a pride in their historical accomplishments. To be left with stripped earth, without the opportunity to gaze at the magnificent feats of their ancestors, made the mainland Chinese feel dishonored.

Recognizing the vast importance of reestablishing their historical and cultural links with their forefathers, the Communist government has adopted a policy under which every one of the country's 950 million citizens acts as a part-time archaeologist. Using Mao Tse-tung's slogan, "Let the Past Serve the Present," Chinese have been taught to be constantly on the lookout for artifacts, how to recognize them, how and where to report their discoveries, and the type of precautions to take until the experts arrive on the scene. As a result, China is beginning to rediscover its rich historical heritage, this time not from Chiang's booty, but from hitherto unknown treasure now being discovered by China's citizens.

Some very important finds have been made in China since the 1960s which testify to the prosperity and opulence that characterized ancient China, although an assessment of the discoveries indicates that some things really haven't changed all that much. This was the case when a post-mortem was conducted on the remains of the Marchioness of Tai, two thousand years after her burial. Despite her wealth and exalted position in Chinese society, the medical examination revealed that she had died of a heart attack, brought on by overeating! Her stomach still showed the remains of no fewer than 138 melon seeds!

She would still be buried in her quiet tomb had it not been for the watchful eyes of the workmen who were digging a foundation for a new hospital at Mawang-tui near Hunan in 1971. Stumbling on an unknown obstruction, they stopped their work and called for assistance. The hastily summoned archaeologist uncovered a grave containing a hexagonal wooden coffin insulated by a thick charcoal jacket that was so tightly sealed off with china clay that it had kept the body in a near-perfect state of preservation ever since its burial in 150 B.C. With her short, stocky build, deformed back, and undoubtedly wobbly gait, the Marchioness had been no raving beauty when she died at fifty years of age; but, thanks to the excitement created by her exhumation, she will go down in the annals of modern archaeological history as a major discovery. Ironically, she herself was only a minor part of the excitement generated by the finding of her grave. Her casket was unique indeed, and the 162 wooden figurines that had been placed in her tomb to accompany her to the spiritual realm also earned their share of the attention. Even her carefully selected wardrobe, checked and inventoried on slips of bamboo, was not the focal point of the find. The real excitement came with the finding of some fifty-odd rolls of some of the finest silk ever to come to us out of ancient China. Stored in basket-weave boxes and, remarkably, in a perfect state of preservation thanks to the dry atmosphere in the tomb, the finely woven bolts and the fabric used in her exquisite wardrobe present modern-day China with an unmatched example of the elegant apparel worn by ladies of rank in Imperial China.

Commented a spokesman for the People's Democratic Republic of China, "The fact that the lady's husband used so much labor and wealth for the burial of his wife shows how brutally the feudal ruling class oppressed and exploited the laboring people." A cynical remark befitting the philosophy of the present government of the country. I sometimes wonder how the same spokesman must have felt three years later when, in the spring of 1974, peasants and workers digging for a well in the Lin-t-'ung district accidentally stumbled on part of a huge underground vault that eventually led to what may be the greatest archaeological find of the century—and perhaps of all times.

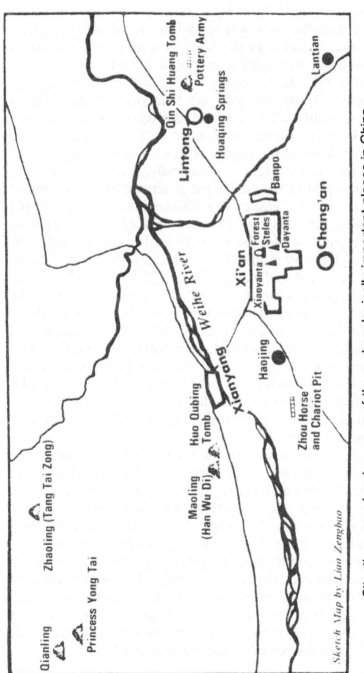

Situation map showing some of the archaeologically important places in China, including the tomb of the First Emperor, Chi'n Shi Huang Ti, and his pottery army.

The area is of great importance fo China, for it was here that the country's earliest emperors lived and died. Hundreds of imperial tombs are hidden beneath the picturesque landscape, each one of them filled with art treasures and riches: a virtual archaeologist's paradise. But because of Red China's preoccupation with maintaining its political system and the development of its industry, very little of it has been excavated.

For many years China's historians have been eager to check out the accuracy of a report found in the works of the great Chinese chronicler Suma Chien, who in 100 B.C. wrote, "As soon as the First Emperor became king of Ch'in, excavations and building had been started at Mount Li, while after he won the empire, more than 700,000 conscripts from all parts of the country worked there. They dug through three underground rivers and poured molten copper for the outer coffin, and the tomb was filled with models of palaces, pavilions, and offices, as well as fine vessels, precious stones and rare items. Artisans were instructed to set up crossbows so that any robber breaking in would be killed. All the rivers of the country, the Yellow River and the Yangtze, were reproduced in quicksilver and made to flow into a miniature ocean through some mechanical means. Even the North Star and the constellations of the heavens were set in precious stones and set in a great copper dome above, while the regions of the earth were also shown. Candles made of whale oil were lit to ensure their burning for the longest possible time."

Fascinating tale; fascinating tomb. But even though its location is known, nothing has ever disturbed its serenity. It stands at a majestic height of 165 feet against the northern foothills of Mount Li in the Wei River valley of China's Kansu province. But as staggering as its reported riches may be, there has always been an unspoken reluctance on the part of China's authorities to enter Chi'n Shi

Huang Ti's tomb. Can it be that despite the harsh exterior of the Chinese communistic structure, traditional ancestor worship has not totally vanished from the scene? The fifteen-story-high mound of earth is overgrown with a protective blanket of trees and blossoming wildflowers, as if nature itself is attempting to hide the naked burial mound from inquisitive eyes. The first emperor's sleep has not been disturbed for more than 2,200 years, but measures are now being taken to penetrate his peaceful grave.

History has its own way of springing surprises on us at the most unexpected moment, as was confirmed by the perchance discovery of an underground vault by a group of Chinese peasants a mile west of the emperor's tomb. The investigation that followed the announcement of their find soon began to reaffirm what had been hinted at by the ancient historical reports. The tomb complex of Chi'n Shi Huang Ti was not confined to the terrain immediately surrounding the gravesite but extended far beyond the fifteen-story mound. Archaeologists are now certain that the unexpected probe will lead them into the most extensive dig ever undertaken by an archaeological team, and that it will prove conclusively that the tomb was the center of an entire "spirit city," an area enclosing prayer temples, sacred stone tablets detailing the virtues of the emperor, and other inscriptions relating his accomplishments. Archaeologists believe that, enclosed within a walled square a quarter of a mile on each side, the inner spirit city was in turn surrounded by an "outer city" with a radius of four miles.

The historical background of the building of the tomb complex is perhaps as startling as what is being found. As soon as the future emperor ascended the throne at age thirteen and his mad rush for conquest of the neighboring kingdoms began, he also started planning his tomb, believing that after death he would rule the entire universe as he had ruled the earth. He fought for twenty-five years of life; lived in relative peace for another eleven years—but spent all thirty-six of them planning for his demise.

During his lifetime Chi'n Shi Huang Ti conquered all of China—in the words of the ancient Chinese historian Suma Chien, like "a silkworm devouring a mulberry leaf." Using the labor of thousands of prisoners and exiled Confucian scholars who were in total opposition to his overthrowing of the ancient ways, he expanded and connected the fragmentary ramparts that had been erected by feudal kings, forging them into the 1,500-mile-long Great Wall of China, a wall sufficiently wide to allow six horses to gallop abreast along the top. It was a ruthless building campaign in which the bones of the thousands who died during its construction were mixed with the mortar, giving the wall the well-earned name of the "longest cemetery on earth."

Today we are able to enjoy the legacies of the emperor's reign *and* his death, for both are well represented in the discoveries that are now being made in China. Soon after the well-diggers stumbled on the underground vault and handed their spades over to the archaeologists, the emperor's honor guard began to stick their heads through the sand—not in the form of broken bones or skeletons, but in life-size ceramic figures rendered in realistic detail. In each new area examined by the team, more terra cotta warriors were uncovered, exposed to the light of the sun for the first time in more than 2,200 years. They were all there: six-foot-tall sculptures of the emperor's warriors and servants, and replicas of their horses—all members of the imperial guard, vigilant and protective of the emperor's body. The faint traces of paint that still cling to the statues indicate that every one of them had been painted in its natural color and marked with the appropriate military rank or social standing.

In 1981 the excavations which had begun in 1974 entered a new stage when the diggers reached the western

Part of Emperor Chi'n Shi Huang Ti's six-thousand-man terra cotta honor guard.

There is no doubt that each warrior in the emperor's army represented a real-life soldier, for they are all different. Sketched here is a general of the army of Emperor Chi'n Shi Huang Ti.

Terra cotta soldiers of the emperor's army being cleaned by a Chinese archaeologist (*right*) and interested peasants. The project is so gigantic that it takes a lot of untrained labor to help unearth the honor guard.

side of the inner wall of the formerly roofed over area that housed the emperor's 6,000-man guard. There archaeologists unearthed two bronze chariots—with charioteers—each drawn by four bronze horses. Probes of the area have indicated that additional formations of ceramic soldiers are still buried, lined up in precisely the way they arrayed themselves before going into battle for the emperor.

While only a few of the eleven corridors presumed to be filled with men and horses have been excavated thus far, new surprises are encountered daily. It is now speculated that the vault may still contain hundreds more bronze horse-and-chariot teams. If this is true, and the princes, court officials, and possibly even the empress were "duplicated" in bronze and placed on the bronze chariots to accompany the emperor in death, then how about their jewelry? May we then expect to find that they are adorned with the exquisite jewelry, precious stones and ornaments worn by their living counterparts?

China's ancient history is coming to life in a strange sort of way, in spite of the loss of the valuable museum pieces taken to Formosa at the time of the Communist takeover. Yet the uncovering of the life-size 6,000-man Imperial Guard of Chi'n Shi Huang Ti is only a foretaste of what promises to be hidden within the tumulus of the emperor itself, which still remains untouched and holding on to its 2,200-year-old secrets. Suma Chien's detailed description of the construction and opulence of the tomb hints at relics so indescribably beautiful that the Chinese archaeologists just don't dare think that far ahead. All the splendor of gold and precious stones ever discovered anywhere else will undoubtedly fade into insignificance when the Chinese begin to inch their way into the burial place of their first emperor.

The work conducted at the foot of Mount Li points up once again the Chinese preoccupation with immortality; when it wasn't being expressed by honoring the memories of their ancestors, it was directed toward the future in the making of preparations for the survival of their own corruptible bodies. Not every Chinese had the opportunity or the resources to make such preparations, but these measures were the rule rather than the exception among the members of the ruling classes.

One failed attempt at preserving bodies for the hereafter became known when workmen dug into the side of a low cliff ninety miles from Peking and discovered a chamber cut into the rocks containing the remains of the Princess Tau Wan, a lady who joined her ancestors over two thousand years ago. Her corpse had deteriorated to nothing more than a mere pinch of dust.

To protect her against the onslaught of the ages, loving hands had dressed her in a funerary suit consisting of a total of 2,156 separate plaques of handcrafted jade, held together by twenty-four ounces of gold wire. A gilded bronze headrest elaborately enhanced with jade had been placed under her head to allow her to rest more comfortably. Ironically, the suit that was to guarantee her survival into eternity had remained totally intact.

Her husband's eternal fate was no better. Given a similar burial in a cave near hers, Prince Liu Sheng was all but gone. A piece of a tooth was found amidst the remains of a disjointed suit similar to that of his wife.

Their graves caused a sensation in China when their jade suits and lavish funerary gifts were discovered in 1968. The old Chinese belief that a covering of jade would preserve the human body forever had finally received its *coup de grâce*.

CHAPTER 6

The Ancient Halls of Record

As a former newsman I have the odd habit of using certain historical years like coat hangers—I hang fond memories upon them. Nineteen fifty-six was one of those memorable years, for it brings back vivid recollections of my first visit to the pyramids of Egypt.

I had just returned to Heidelberg, Germany, where I had done a story about the Red Ball Express, a U.S. Army truck convoy that hauled equipment and supplies over long distances. I was becoming fed up with the dreary office routine at our European headquarters of the *Soldier Illustrated* when in November the French, British and Israelis launched their surprise attack on a vastly outnumbered Egyptian force.

Eager to get out of the routine, I dumped the job of running the office into someone else's lap, grabbed my cameras and field gear, hastily cut a set of travel orders, and climbed aboard the next military flight heading for the Middle East to cover the war. Since I was going in on the Allied side and the Egyptians were notoriously poor shots, I thought it a safe territory for correspondents.

The eventual outcome of the 1956 conflict is ancient history now, but the contacts I made that fall—both professionally and socially—still evoke an occasional chuckle. It was there that I met Mohammed Fauzy, and with him as a guide I roamed about the dark corridors of the pyramids and gazed in quiet fascination at the Sphinx. And it was there too that I heard the first whispered rumors about a hidden library and a secret temple supposedly still concealed somewhere underneath the desert sands.

We were lazily slouched down in a stack of soft wool pillows one evening in a corner of the old circus tent known as the Gizereh Nightclub, romantically situated near a cluster of date palms within viewing distance of the Great Pyramid, when Mohammed first mentioned the story to me. Since he was well known as Egypt's most popular singer of romantic ballads, people flocked to him to ask for his financial backing for their wildest schemes, hoping he'd be willing to get involved. Finding a secret underground temple was one scheme that tempted him.

"About two years ago, an old Druzean friend of mine came to me and asked for my help," he confided, trying to make his whisper heard above the sound of the Egyptian band that accompanied the gyrating motions of the belly dancer in front of us. "There is a persistent rumor among the Druzes that somewhere close to the Sphinx there is an underground temple of unknown origin that forms the entrance to a secret library of ancient knowledge. A sort of 'history of the world' of predawn times . . . .

"I'm a singer"—Mohammed smiled—"but I am a businessman above all, and I told him that I'd be glad to see what I could do to help, but that he would have to give me more information than just that! We talked for another five minutes before he left, promising to return the next day with more details, including specific information about the location of the temple.

"You know what? He never did! Not that day or the

next. It was a full three days later that someone told me in passing that the man he had seen me talking to had been killed, run down by a car in downtown Alexandria . . . .''

I looked at him questioningly. "Do you see any connection between the story and his death?"

Mohammed held up his hands in a gesture of helplessness. "How do I know? . . . Inshallah . . . inshallah . . . the Lord willing . . . the will of Allah be done," he intoned softly, nervously fingering his yellow worry beads. "Who knows? Here one never knows . . . "

Many years and several wars have passed since I listened to Mohammed's whispered rumor about the hidden temple. Little did I know that the ancient library, later also referred to as the "Hall of Records," would eventually be much sought after by psychic archaeologists.

In writing books on psychics *(Jeane Dixon—My Life & Prophecies, You Are Psychic,* and *The Soul Hustlers),* I had sometimes stumbled on vague references to secret libraries that were supposed to contain vast amounts of historical, cultural and occult information. But while the psychics often alluded to their existence, they seldom furnished any additional details as to the location of these depositories. Finding a hidden storehouse of ancient knowledge, however, would be a major scientific discovery, since the rampaging armies of old have destroyed most of the great libraries of the ancient world. Many of history's missing pages were torn out in those calamitous years.

The famous collection of Pisastratus (Pisander) in Athens (sixth century B.C.) was ravaged. The papyri of the library of the Temple of Ptah in Memphis in Egypt were totally destroyed. The same fate befell 200,000 volumes in the library of Pergamus in Asia Minor. The city of Carthage, razed by the Romans in a seventeen-day fire in 146 B.C., is said to have possessed a library of close to half a million volumes. But the greatest blow to history was probably the burning of the Alexandrian library during the Egyptian campaign of Julius Caesar, when 700,000 priceless scrolls were lost. There was even a complete catalogue of authors in 120 volumes, with a brief biography of each author. The library building itself, however, somehow survived the destruction and once again became a center of learning, the most important book depository until Omar, the second Caliph of Islam, used its millions of book rolls to heat the city's bathing facilities in A.D. 640. For six long months the fires roared, fueled by the knowledge of the ancients. The few voices that could be heard in protest were quickly silenced by the caliph. "The contents of the books are in conformity with the Koran or they are not," he ruled. "If they are, the Koran is sufficient without them. If they are not, they are pernicious. Let them therefore be burned."

The fate of the libraries in Asia was no better, for Emperor Ch'in Shi Huang Ti of China caused all historical books to be burned in 212 B.C., while Leo Isaurus sent 300,000 books to the incinerators of Constantinople in the eighth century. There is no way to estimate the number of manuscripts destroyed by the fanatics of the Inquisition during the Middle Ages, and for much of our understanding we have to rely on disconnected fragments, casual passages, and meager accounts. The history of science and of the development of nations would appear totally different were the books of the library of Alexandria still intact today.

Historians are well aware of this mass destruction, yet aside from a few educated guesses, no one really knows the full extent of the knowledge that was so recklessly destroyed. Would it have disclosed advanced technology of ancient nations? Did it contain detailed information about their concepts and developments of medicine, physics, interstellar communications, biology, and other fields of science in which we believe modern man excels? And how about computerization? Unconfirmed sources keep referring to so-called occult libraries within the Vatican and valuable scroll collections that are reputed to be in the possession of secret organizations such as the Masonic lodges. But men who claim to know, like the mysterious Dr. Trauger, a Southern California physician who had climbed to the highest degree in occult Masonry, don't talk. A wearer of a special ring that had come to him from an occult Mason in India, he was a true master of the occult sciences. His was the realm of darkness. He even conducted his medical practice during the nighttime hours, sleeping the day away. Accompanied by his retinue of black cats, he'd roam through his rambling Los Angeles house at night until he grew desperate in his loneliness. We originally met through a KFI radio program and stayed in touch for many years. I still remember his late-evening and early-morning calls and his frantic need for a "sounding board." His occult knowledge was beginning to spill over, as if his memory had been filled to the brim. Yet he always stopped himself short when he began to allude to his strange dark world.

Before a particular trip, I stored a trunk full of Egyptology books in his basement. When I returned half a year later and went to "Doc's" house to collect them, I found that his name was no longer on his door—and he was gone.

"He died—quite suddenly," I was informed by one of the neighbors. "It was just as if he disappeared overnight." And with him disappeared his ring and another door to one of the few remaining caches of ancient occult knowledge. Even though he once hinted that he alone could open doors for me that would remain closed to everyone else, he disappeared without opening them so much as a crack.

Because of all this, Mohammed Fauzy's mention of an underground temple and library had a familiar sound to it. But with the death of his Druzean friend this leak of ancient information too was plugged.

Yet psychics have a way of picking up information that seems to escape everyone else; and long before my meetings with "Doc" and Mohammed Fauzy's encounter with the Druze, Edgar Cayce, one of the world's leading psychics, tapped into a source of psychic power that pointed unhesitantly toward the elusive "Hall of Records."

During his lifetime, Cayce gave more than 14,000 "readings" (psychic insights) on a variety of subjects, including medicine and history. Much of his early "historical" work is closely related to the downfall of the imaginary and/or legendary continent of Atlantis, whose history, culture and scientific achievements are allegedly recorded in secret subterranean vaults.

What ties his psychic predictions in with the rumors of the Druze is the approximate location his "spiritual source" gives for the sacred temple: within the immediate vicinity of the Great Pyramid and the Sphinx! It appears now that psychic archaeology had its beginnings way back in the 1930s when Edgar Cayce received his first message about the hidden chambers of antiquity, and not with Stephen Schwartz and his organization's discoveries in the harbor of Alexandria—although Schwartz did put theory and insight into practice.

It comes as no surprise that someone has connected a "prehistoric" temple complex and a library with the Great Pyramid and the Sphinx. The Cheops pyramid has been a center of intense controversy ever since it was first seen by Westerners, and even more so since the appearance of the book *The Great Pyramid, Its Divine Message,* written by D. Davidson and H. Aldersmith and published in 1924. A rare combination of fiction, wishful thinking, folklore, and misinterpreted ancient history, the book was a masterful attempt to find within the pyramid a prophecy of world events, complete with dates. The work was not

original by any means; it was built on earlier works by
John Taylor (*The Great Pyramid: Why Was It Built? And
Who Built It?* 1839) and Charles Piazzi Smyth, the astron-
omer-royal of Scotland whose 1867 three-volume work
entitled *Life and Work at the Great Pyramid* was a formi-
dable classic of ignorance and speculation. But whether
based on truth or on fiction, the books contained sufficient double-talk to envelop the pyramid in a cloud of
mystery. Add to this the sense of romance inherent in the
Middle East—Bedouins, smoky water pipes, loping camels and lush oases—and the massive structure was des-
tined to remain a focal point of historical suspense for
years to come. And as one of the Seven Wonders of the
World, the Great Pyramid has long been the object of
spurious speculation, and over the years more has been
written about it than about any other man-made structure
on the face of the earth.

Aside from the baffling occult riddles it may or may
not present, its measurements are truly impressive.
Located ten miles west of the old and historic city of
Cairo, it is thought to have been built as the tomb of the
Pharaoh Cheops, albeit his remains were never found
there. The huge pyramid covers a little over thirteen acres
and measures 760 feet at each baseline and 481 feet in
height. The Great Pyramid is constructed entirely of
stone—huge blocks of yellow limestone weighing as much
as fifty-four tons each. In geometric form, it is a true pyramid. Its base is a perfect square; each of its four sides is
a perfect equilateral triangle which slants evenly inward
and upward from the base. The bearings of the base with
respect to true east, west, north and south show an error
of only five seconds—far and away the most accurately
oriented building known to engineering science today.

Not far from the Great Pyramid lies the lone figure of
the Sphinx, the stone image of a lion's body with a human
head, still partially adorned with an Egyptian headdress.

Measuring 189 feet in length, it was cut out of one single block of stone which was obviously not indigenous to the area. It is a representation of the god Horus and is thought to predate the Great Pyramid by many years, although there is no conclusive proof for this position.

The origin and meaning of both the Pyramid and the Sphinx have always been rather cloudy, but that they had a dominant function in the occult practices of the Egyptian or even pre-Egyptian priesthood is a distinct possibility.

In western Europe, where national boundaries have often changed but the basic scenery has remained relatively untouched by the passing of the years, much of what lies underneath the surface can be detected by the use of high-altitude photography with electronic photo enhancement. In the Middle East, specifically in areas where the rains and sandstorms have played their seasonal games uninterruptedly year after year, century after century, for thousands of years, fertile plains have been transformed into deserts, and meadows have been buried under billions of tons of ever-shifting sand. There the remnants of civilizations that once ruled the world have gently been laid to rest under a deep layer of sand. As a result, aerial photography is not always so successful in locating buried tombs and other structures in the Middle East as it is in Europe. That is precisely why Cayce's insight into the history of Egypt may be of such tremendous help.

Today's psychics lean heavily on the insight of two people for their prophetic accuracy quotient: Nostradamus, the sixteenth-century French astrologer and prognosticator, and Edgar Cayce. Without them most psychics would not dare go very far into the future with their predictions on world affairs, even though they hate to admit their utter dependence on these two psychic greats. This may explain why the psychics who have alluded to a secret vault somewhere under the desert sands of Egypt haven't gotten too specific for fear of sounding like Edgar Cayce.

All of Cayce's information concerning the vault is closely interwoven with references to the Atlantians and their history, which he claims will be brought to light when the Hall of Records is finally opened. He looks upon the hidden library as a sort of time capsule that will reveal to us the "precious" records of Atlantian "originals," including detailed information about their scientific achievements, their literature, history and laws, and their treatises on "the abilities to use the unseen forces."

In his writings Cayce makes scores of allusions to a future opening of this Hall of Records, which he says is contained in a small pyramid of its own. In one book on the subject, the seer claims that the people who had gathered and compiled the sacred records were buried alongside their artifacts, which will provide meaningful evidence of their existence. Included in the buried items are such things as harps, lyres, lutes, and violas. He furthermore claims that there will also be found the "hangings, the accoutrements for the altar in the temple of the day," and the "cymbals for the calling of the people to worship." He also mentions the possibility of finding gold and precious stones used for healing and exchange and surgical instruments, as well as various medications.

If Edgar Cayce is correct—and his millions of followers have no doubt of it—then the Hall of Records is indeed a true treasure house of both knowledge *and* artifacts. "Caskets of gold, or the golden bands about those whose bodies were put into the burial chambers," will be discovered, according to the seer; but whereas many of his forecasts deal specifically with the Hall of Records, he also makes mention of a "mound not yet uncovered" where a king has been buried surrounded by his personal belongings. Whether this "mound" or pyramid is part of the "temple city" that is supposed to lie just beyond the

Great Pyramid he did not say. But he did point out that when it is uncovered, many of the shrines will be found to display inscriptions to the goddess Isssi.

Cayce was not only a psychic but also a deeply religious man, and his views about the origin of man often found a place in his readings. Talking about the sacred Hall, he once commented,

"[In this chamber] . . . is a record of Atlantis from the beginnings of those periods when the Spirit took form or began the encasements in that land, and the developments of the peoples throughout their sojourn, with the record of the first destruction and the changes that took place in the land, with the record of the sojourning of the peoples to the varied activities in other lands, and a record of the meetings of all the nations or lands for the activities in the destruction that became necessary, with the final destruction of Atlantis and the building of the pyramid of initiation, with who, what, where, would come the opening of the records that are as copies from the sunken Atlantis; for with the change it must rise again . . . "

A lengthy and rambling comment indeed, but the psychic master could also be very specific, and this ability was displayed when he later wrote out the location of the ancient Hall of Records. He described the site of this spectacular structure as follows:

"This in position lies, as the sun rises from the waters, the line of the shadow falls between the paws of the Sphinx, that was later set as the sentinel or guard, and which may not be entered from the connecting chambers from the Sphinx's paw until the time has been fulfilled when the changes must be active in the sphere of man's experience. Between, then, the Sphinx and the river."

And ever since that time, adventurers and the more serious-minded researchers have often thought of putting Cayce's prophecy to the test by attempting an on-site investigation. Atlantis has always been regarded either as a figment of someone's fruitful imagination or as a product of mythology; and because the stories about it rested on no foundation whatsoever, science has never accepted even the possibility of its existence. Thus the task of proving anything at all about the Atlantians is left to the amateurs.

One man who took Edgar Cayce's words about Atlantis seriously was his son Hugh Lynn, who in 1972 began to move in the direction of finding support for his father's readings. He knew that if they could be proved to be true, and the Hall of Records and the temple city could indeed be found, it would become necessary to rewrite the history of the world.

After various tests, Hugh Lynn Cayce and a Canadian "sensitive," George McMullen, accompanied by a group of friends, headed for Egypt in October 1975 to check out some of the elder Cayce's observations. Stephen A. Schwartz refers to this trip in *The Secret Vaults of Time.*

"Of great significance were his perceptions regarding the Sphinx and the Giza Plain," he writes. "There he outlined underground and as yet undiscovered water systems, pointing out the locations of channels, pools, fountains in an area that had been largely overlooked by Egyptologists—although drilling in front of the Sphinx earlier had hit water."

While scouting the area around the Sphinx, McMullen made another significant observation. Ever since the early 1700s, when the Englishman Thomas Shaw had climbed his way to the top of the Sphinx and found a hole in its head, European scholars had wondered whether the hole might not indicate the absence of something that had once occupied that space. Eventually the consensus was reached that that "something" must have been a crown, but since there are no pictures available anywhere of a Sphinx-with-a-crown, its shape and size have remained the subject of speculation.

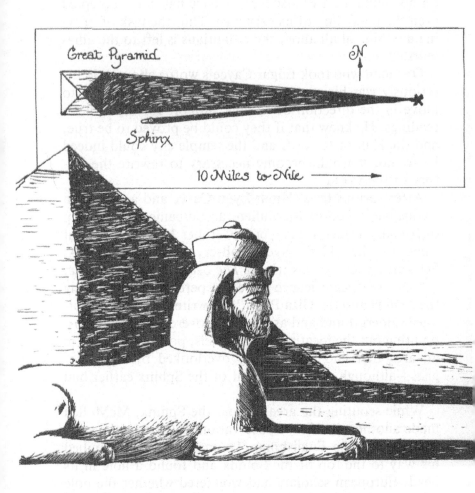

According to the psychics, the Hall of Records will be found at the spot where the shadows of the Great Pyramid and the Head of the Sphinx meet "on a day late in October as the sun sets."

McMullen, however, not only averred that there had been a crown, but also described its shape and gave its specific dimensions to his fellow travelers.

Further, the Great Pyramid originally had a capstone, according to McMullen, and before any questions could be asked, he gave its dimensions as seen from his psychic viewpoint. He furnished just enough information to complete the partial instructions originally supplied by Edgar Cayce. With his vision as a guide, the Hall could be located *"on a day late in October as the sun sets, [when] the shadow cast by the Cheops Pyramid and by the head of the Sphinx—allowing for the crown and the capstone— will overlap, merge, and coincide at a single point on the flat pavement-like plaza area in the direction of the Nile."*

Fascinating information indeed, and undoubtedly of great value for anyone planning to throw all doubt to the wind, dig for the vault, and come up with the greatest discovery of the century. But can it *really* be all that simple? Even though George McMullen was on the site in 1975, does that mean that he "saw" a shadow being cast in that same year, or was it a shadow cast thousands of years earlier, at the time when both the Sphinx and the Great Pyramid stood there in all their glory? Also, does his psychic view take into consideration the shifts in the earth's axis, differences in terrain elevation, other buildings whose shadows might interfere, or any of a hundred other variables? And even though the crown and the capstone respectively seem to complete the two structures, Cayce did not specify whether their addition should be considered in the calculations. Without the missing objects, the shadows cast will be much shorter and less well defined, for they will certainly not converge in a single point.

Perhaps the time has come for science to take over, the psychics having shown their limitations. Astronomers can help in determining the shifts in the earth's axis during the last, let's say, seven thousand years. They can also work out the lengths and the exact placement of the two shadows and their point of overlapping and merging, both with and without crown and capstone, since in both cases we know the height of the objects. In narrowing the target area down to a certain number of square miles (remember that the distance between the Great Pyramid and the Nile is less than ten miles), high-resolution aerial photography with electronic enhancement might be of some help. Electrical resistivity soundings will also have to be employed in this locating process, as well as conventional probing.

But while the search for the Egyptian Hall of Records is still in the psychic stage, with sensitives attempting to gather more information, other psychics are now beginning to focus their attention on Latin America, where other civilizations have left their remains.

South America once was a cultural paradise—at least until the Spanish began to take possession of it. From the moment the conquistador Francisco Pizarro led his 177 men into the Peruvian highlands from San Miguel in September 1532, the bells began to toll for the demise of the Inca empire. A short two months after their invasion, the armed band reached Caajamarca and encountered the Inca ruler Atahualpa, who had just defeated Huáscar in a civil war. Taking him prisoner in a daring ambush, they held him hostage until he had paid his ransom—enough gold and silver to fill a room in the palace to the height of a man's reach—after which the Spaniards garroted him anyway. Various uprisings by the Incas sought to break the increasing hold of the Spanish on their land, but their resistance as a nation finally ended in 1572, when Tupa Amaru, the last Inca, was beheaded in Cuzco, and the remnants of the proud nation withdrew into the inaccessible mountains.

What had started as a small kingdom around Cuzco around A.D. 1200 had grown into a magnificent empire that ranged all the way from Quito, Ecuador, in the north

Francisco Pizarro, conquistador and murderer of nations, conquered the Incas and made for himself a lasting name in the history of the world. (Archivo General de Indias, Seville, Spain)

to Chile in the south. At the pinnacle of its glory it stretched more than 2,500 miles from north to south and included half of present-day Bolivia and part of north-western Argentina. Yet 177 Spaniards and the unquench-able thirst for gold of the conquistadores destroyed it all.

Ever since the Incan empire's golden shine faded away into the darkness of time, the tales about its riches have grown, and the great museums in Peru, Ecuador, Colom-bia and Chile house more gold and silver artifacts of the Inca empire than they do of anything else. But judging from the numbers of ancient gold objects the Indians keep bringing in, there is more, much more, to be had.

But where is it? By now it is obvious that the conquista-dores did not succeed in stripping the Inca empire of all its gold, and much of it disappeared into the mountain strongholds. But Francisco Pizarro cannot be blamed for that—nor can his brother Hernando, who often resorted to torture when he did not find what he expected.

Not being able to amass treasure as fast as he had hoped, Hernando began to send his men out on specific missions with specific goals. On one of these "search and destroy" missions he sent one man to plunder Jauja and others to rob Cuzco's Temple of the Sun. Both raids were highly successful.

The Negro who had been sent to Jauja returned with 107 loads of gold and seven of silver; while Cuzco's Tem-ple of the Sun enriched the Spaniards with 285 loads of precious metal for a total of more than twenty-four tons by mid-1533. The stolen treasure consisted of idols, chal-ices, necklaces, nuggets, fountains, golden vessels, drink-ing cups, dismantled altars, and ceremonial plaques. In the annals of those raids it is recorded that nine blazing fires were required to reduce the priceless creations to lumps of gleaming metal. As a result of these theft excur-sions, each soldier who took part received forty-five pounds of gold and ninety pounds of silver. Cavalrymen received two shares each, De Soto four shares, and Hernando Pizarro seven, while the governor was rewarded with thirteen shares as well as Atahualpa's 200-pound golden litter.

But even today, the question remains: Is there still more? And if so, where is it?

For years historians and archaeologists have been telling us that even though the Incas had a highly developed society, the art of writing was unknown to them and that they had no written history. Accounts of the area are based mainly on information compiled by chroniclers of the conquistadores. Is it perhaps possible that somewhere in the Andes mountains there are vaults of Incan treasure secreted away before the Spaniards could lay their hands on it—and that along with this treasure some form of history of the South American continent may still be found?

The terror that engulfed the hearts of the Incas when they were confronted with the unmitigated cruelty of the Spanish conquistadores and the fear that gripped them when they saw their emperor garroted must have made them realize that their traditional way of living was coming to an end. The Spaniards' obvious thirst for gold and their quest for the golden Inca gods must have impelled the natives to start hiding their precious objects right from the very outset of the conflict. If there existed any written records, historical material or inscriptions testifying to the origin of their civilization, they may well have secreted them along with their gold. If so, the old Inca region may yet produce some surprises.

That we need a new find of South American chronicles no historian will deny, for most of what had been found in South America in years past has since been destroyed. In 1549 when Diego de Landa, an overzealous young monk, discovered a large library of Mayan codices in Mexico, his religious fanaticism got the upper hand. "We burned them all because they contained nothing except superstition and the machinations of the devil!'' he wrote proudly, recalling his dastardly destructive act. How could he possibly have known what the books contained, since he was totally unable to read them? When de Landa had grown older and wiser and had finally received the title of bishop, he realized what he had done, and he made a frantic search for additional Mayan inscriptions— but to no avail.

There is, however, a tradition that fifty-two golden tablets containing the history of Central America are still preserved somewhere in a temple, carefully concealed there by the Aztec priests before the greedy conquistadores reached Tenochtitlán.

If one had gone to the Madrid Library a hundred years ago and requested a copy of the *First New Chronicle and Good Government* by Felipe Huaman Poman de Ayala, dated 1565, the librarian would have shrugged her shoulders and sent him on, for at that time no one had ever heard of a book by that name. The manuscript for that history of the Incas lay in total obscurity for centuries, until it eventually turned up in the Royal Library in Copenhagen, Denmark, in 1908. It was published for the first time in 1927 and is now considered as good a source of Inca history as is Carcilaso de la Vega's or the one written by Cieza de Leon. Yet this is only one of many chronicles that have turned up. Is it possible that more written manuscripts about the ancient races are yet to be found? We still know too little about our past to be able to assess it accurately. New finds may solve some unexplained mysteries, and the reading of ancient narratives, if found, might turn much of our accepted history of certain areas of the world upside down.

There is no denying that more wisdom has been lost than preserved during our earth's catastrophic history. For example, there is supposed to have existed a series of books in South America that contained all the basic wisdom of antiquity; but it was destroyed by Pachacuti IV, one of the Inca rulers, because it contradicted his own beliefs. In this case, we will probably never know whether we are dealing with fact or fiction or some of both, for history has its own odd way of so masquerading and distorting facts that in the course of years they often lose all association with reality.

We do know that with man's unquenchable thirst for adventure and for discovery of new frontiers, the boundaries of our knowledge are continually being pushed back. The Spaniards—even though they collected hundreds of millions of dollars' worth of gold and silver in Peru— never accepted for one moment that the gold and silver objects surrendered to them were all the conquered Incas possessed. When Francisco Pizarro carried his search into the mountains, he discovered cave entrances closed with heavy slabs of rock on Huascaran, the "Mountain of the Incas." Finding it impossible to remove the slabs, the angry Spaniard engaged in all sorts of speculation as to what might be hidden behind them; but in the end he had to retreat, empty-handed and frustrated, for the rocks would not yield their secrets to the Spanish.

It was not until 1971 that the slabs were finally forced out of the way to allow entry to an expedition that went down into the dark void behind the gaping opening. Using modern equipment such as winches, lamps, oxygen tanks, etc., they descended to a depth of two hundred feet, where they discovered a series of connecting caves. A short distance into the caves, the men found their progress blocked by what appeared to be watertight doors made of huge slabs of rock. Examining them closely, they realized that the "primitive" engineers who had been responsible for installing doors had placed their edges on stone balls lying in a shallow pool formed by dripping water. It took one good push—and the doors opened!

Reports the German scientific quarterly, *Bild der Wissenschaft,* published in Stuttgart:

"Long tunnels which would be the envy of modern subterranean construction engineers began right behind the six doors. The tunnels headed straight for the coast, sometimes at an angle of 14 percent. The tunnel floor was covered with slabs of stone that had been made slip proof by pitting and grooving them. Even today it is a real adventure to follow these 55–65-mile-long tunnels and end up 80 feet below sea level; and imagine the problems that must have been encountered during the fourteenth and fifteenth centuries when they were used to transport goods deep under the Andes in order to save them from the grasp of Pizarro and the Spanish Viceroy.

"After the tunnels have gone uphill and downhill several times in deep darkness, the murmur and strangely hollow sounding noise of surf is heard. In the searchlight the next downhill slip ends on the edge of a pitch black flood which is identified as sea water. The present-day coast also begins here underground. Was this perhaps not the case in former times?"

It is speculated that these passages once led to Guanape, an island that lies off the coast of Peru.

No one really knows for sure whether the tunnels did lead to Guanape, but tradition has it that after the murder of Atahualpa his successor let it quietly be known that all the empire's treasures were to be collected and hidden in the subterranean tunnel system, there to await better times. But the successor too died, and the secret died with him—and the priests who were in on the plan never talked.

Yet the hiding of their treasures presents us with more mysteries than just the disappearance of what may well have been vast quantities of gold and silver. The expedition as described in *Bild der Wissenschaft* discovered an ancient tunnel system that was so precisely cut and had walls so smooth and so well engineered that they testified to a very sophisticated technology and a people with capabilities that far surpassed the known development of the Incas. It was an underground "road" system, a communications network the Incas inherited from the race that preceded them. In many places in Peru, other examples of engineering that may well have been left by the same race still baffle us today.

High in the Andes, on the picturesque shores of Lake Titicaca, stand the remains of a city of startling dimensions—and no one knows its origin. Not even the oldest living Indian would tell of its history when questioned by the Spanish conquistadores in their bloody assault on the area in 1549. Whoever its engineers were, they certainly were not related to the Indians in any way, as the foreign element is quite apparent both from the style of the structures and from the fact that the statues of Tiahuanaco depict strange-looking men with beards—not the usual Indian faces, which tend to be devoid of beard growth.

The society that developed the entire Tiahuanaco area had technical abilities that astounded the conquistadores. Archaeologists who have studied the site since its discovery by the Spaniards have uncovered features thought to be unknown to the ancients. The Akapana, or "Hill of Sacrifices," one of the three important temple sites, was a huge truncated pyramid, 167 feet high, with a base 496 by 650 feet. The now-crumbling sides of the impressive structure were perfectly squared with the cardinal points of the compass, a feature common with other great edifices found around the world, including the Great Pyramid of Gizeh. The destructive plundering of the Spanish conquerors erased some of the clues that might have served as keys to unlock the secrets of the ancient inhabitants, and the ravages of time have deteriorated the rest. Today the side surfaces of the Akapana are rough and torn; the stone slabs that provided a protective cover for the

Archaeologists have discovered many gold ornaments and masks in tombs of ancient peoples such as the Mochicas, who lived in Peru hundreds of years before the Incas ever came on the scene. Pictured here is a gold death mask found on the skull of one of the buried Mochicas. (Museo del Oro, Lima, Peru)

mound have been hauled away to be used in construction projects. The enormous stone stairway that once flanked the hill has also become a victim of gross vandalism. Today, only a few steps remain. The Jesuit historian Bernabe Cobo noted in 1653 that,

"The rumor that great abundance of riches was buried in these buildings has induced some Spaniards to excavate them in search of it and they have found at various times many pieces of gold and silver, though not as much as was thought to be there . . . . They have also despoiled it in order to make use of the stones. For the Church of

Tiahuanaco was built from them and the inhabitants of the town of Chuquiago [La Paz] carried off many to build their houses, and even the Indians in the village of Tiahuanaco make their tombs from beautiful stone tiles which they obtain from the ruins . . . ''

The reservoir system that once topped the Akapana is also indicative of the high degree of technical development of the builders. The hill still reveals evidence of precision-designed, intricately cut stone conduits and overflow pipes, especially graded to ensure proper flow of water. Similar pipes are scattered throughout the Tiahuanaco complex, suggesting that the city had a complete drainage, water supply, or sewage system.

But even the famed Temple of the Sun from which Hernando Pizarro's men took a fortune is definitely not of Inca origin—even though the Incas used it. The temple rests on a stone platform 10 feet high and 440 by 390 feet on a side, composed of blocks weighing one to two hundred tons each! The walls of the temple complex itself are constructed of blocks weighing sixty tons each, while the steps of the stone stairway weigh an impressive fifty tons apiece. Other structural units composed of two-hundred-ton blocks lie haphazardly just where they fell. Tiahuanaco is a place where contradictions and impossibilities reign supreme. Things that can't happen have happened here. It is amazing that the city exists at all; the entire metropolis was built 13,000 feet above sea level, where the air pressure is only eight pounds per square inch, as compared to fifteen pounds per square inch at sea level. The thin, oxygen-poor air sears the nose and throat, and even the slightest exertion may cause nausea, headaches, and sometimes even heart attacks. In addition, no seeds will grow or even sprout at that elevation, which means that there was no local food supply to support a large working crew. Yet somehow, under extremely hostile conditions that threatened life itself, the builders managed to maneuver hundreds of stone slabs weighing up to two hundred tons each into their predetermined places. The quarries from which the stones were taken have been discovered on an island in Lake Titicaca, but near the shore opposite Curicancha. It was therefore necessary to transport the stones over distances ranging from thirty to ninety miles. *In such rarefied air the movement of massive objects over such great distances is not possible by muscular strength alone.*

Tiahuanaco is by no means unique, for scattered throughout the Andes are several fortresses of very similar design, all predating the ancient Incas by an unknown span of time—and all probably built by the same race of men who dug the tunnels that honeycomb the western coastline of South America.

In Chile, high on the plateau of El Enladrillado and well within the borders of the ancient Inca empire, are 233 stone blocks that have been placed geometrically in an amphitheaterlike arrangement. The blocks are roughly rectangular, some as large as twelve to sixteen feet high, twenty to thirty feet long, and weighing several hundred tons. As at Tiahuanaco, huge chairs of stone have also been found in disarray among the ruins, each weighing a massive ten tons. But perhaps the most important find at El Enladrillado was the discovery of three standing stones at the center of the plateau. Each is three to four feet in diameter. Measurements reveal that two of the stones are perfectly aligned with magnetic north, while a line through one of these and the third stone points to the midsummer sunrise . . . .

To the north, at Ollantaytambo, Peru, is another pre-Inca fortress, with rock walls of tightly fitted blocks weighing between 150 and 250 tons each. Most of the blocks consist of very hard andesite, *the quarries for which are situated on a mountaintop seven miles away!* Somehow, at an altitude of 10,000 feet, the unknown builders of Ollantaytambo carved and dressed the stone (using tools the nature of which we can only guess to penetrate such hard rock), lowered the two-hundred-ton blocks down the mountainside, crossed a river canyon with 1,000-foot sheer rock walls, then raised the blocks up another mountainside and placed them in the fortress complex. As South American antiquarian Hyatt Verrill notes, mere men, no matter how many—Indian or otherwise—could not duplicate this feat using only their muscle power and the stone implements or crude metal tools, ropes and rollers that we know about. "It is not a question of skill, patience and time," Verrill explains. "It is a human impossibility." Is it possible that a higher form of prehistoric technology was employed of which we know absolutely nothing?

Let's look at one more example of the "primitive" engineers' capabilities. One of the most impressive "mystery fortresses" of the Andes, Sacsahuaman, is located on the outskirts of the ancient Inca capital of Cuzco. It rests on an artificially leveled mountaintop at an altitude of 12,000 feet and consists of three outer lines of gargantuan walls, 1,500 feet long and 54 feet wide, surrounding a paved area containing a circular stone structure believed to be a solar calendar. The ruins also include a 50,000-gallon water reservoir, storage cisterns, ramps, citadels and underground chambers.

What is truly remarkable, however, about Sacsahuaman is the stonework. Here extremely skilled stonemasons fitted blocks weighing from fifty to three hundred tons into intricate patterns. A block in one of the outer walls, for example, has faces cut to fit perfectly with twelve other blocks. Other blocks were cut with as many as ten, twelve, and even thirty-six sides. Yet all the blocks were fitted together so precisely that a mechanic's thickness gauge could not be inserted between them. And even more extraordinary is the fact that the entire

Sacsahuaman complex was built without cement! As with the other mystery fortresses, the question of how the stones of Sacsahuaman were transported remains unanswered. The quarries from which they were mined are located twenty miles away, on the other side of a mountain range and across a deep river gorge. How the massive stones were moved across such rugged terrain is anyone's guess.

Sacsahuaman poses many mysteries, but there is one in particular which few orthodox historians are willing to recognize or study because of its "impossibility." Within a few hundred yards of the Sacsahuaman complex is a single stone block that was carved from the mountainside and moved some distance before it was abandoned. An earthquake apparently interrupted the progress of the movers, for the stone was turned upside down and damaged in several places. It contains steps, platforms, holes and other depressions—a masterpiece of precision cutting and dressing, clearly intended to become a part of the fortification. What is truly impossible about the block is that it is the size of a five-story house and weighs an estimated 20,000 tons! We have no combination of machinery today that could dislodge such a weight, let alone move it any distance. The fact that the builders of Sacsahuaman could and did move this block shows their mastery of a technology to which we as yet have not attained.

The engineers who were responsible for these nigh-unbelievable structural accomplishments were probably the very same men who carved out the huge systems of interconnected tunnels that extends for hundreds, perhaps thousands of miles under Peru's mountainous terrain, probably linking all its important temples and fortresses into one gigantic civil/religious network. It seems somehow as though they constructed the facilities for an entire underground civilization without those who lived on the surface ever knowing about its existence—except perhaps for the rulers and the priests. Why they built their cities in such impossible places and dug their tunnels at such tremendous depths is still a mystery. But there are indications that all this may soon change. In a notarial deed issued on July 21, 1969, in Guayaquil, Ecuador, Juan Moricz, an Argentine, is listed as the owner of a number of underground caves he reportedly discovered in Ecuador in 1965. The deed also lists what he claims the caves contain.

According to his report, he has discovered a vast network of caves that begin 750 feet underground at the end of a long vertical shaft divided into three floors of 250 feet each. The caves, whose walls reportedly have an almost polished appearance, run for hundreds of miles and end at one point in a large hall. The hall has been described as a huge room furnished with a large table and a number of gigantic chairs made of an unfamiliar stonelike material. Against one of the walls of the room is claimed to be a rack filled with a vast collection of metal plaques inscribed with what he feels may be a condensation of the history of a long-lost civilization, engraved with hieroglyphics in a language unknown to us. He also makes mention of a great number of stone and metal objects and other artifacts which, according to him, constitute a find of great historical and cultural value to mankind.

Truth or fiction—or, again, some of each? It is hard to determine, since a scientific exploration has not yet examined the actual site; yet if there is indeed a prehistoric library of some kind in the subterranean tunnels that were made by the Incas' ancestors, then it certainly deserves a serious investigation. The idea itself is not so fantastic as it might seem, for no nation can really totally vanish without leaving at least a trace of its existence. If the Incas felt the need to create a sophisticated tunnel system to help guarantee their survival, it is not unreasonable to assume that they may have left a "time capsule," a historical record of their accomplishments, their culture, and their political history for their survivors or descendants or for any who would eventually follow in their footsteps.

It is entirely possible that the race of engineers died out thousands of years before the Incas came on the scene, that the Incas' penetration into the tunnel system came too late to be of any help to the survivors of the ancient race. Perhaps they *intended* to be gone totally before another race moved in to occupy their cities and their tunnels, and left Halls of Records to tell the world of their wealth, their accomplishments, their tragedies and their ultimate destruction. They are gone—of that there is no doubt. It is only through their hidden records that they may come back to life, and perhaps issue a warning.

CHAPTER 7

Of Cities and Chariots

It has often been said that the most endearing and perhaps the most valuable qualities that separate humans from the rest of the animal kingdom are our sense of humor and our imagination—though not necessarily in that order.

Although man's grasp of humor is sometimes questionable, man's capacity for dreaming the grand dream has certainly been proved beyond doubt by the great adventurers of times past. Let's face it: it really does not require any humor at all. To start searching for treasure in faraway places demands a vivid imagination; and when we look back at the men who explored the New World—both north and south—we find that they had this one quality in great abundance.

Adventurers they were, and as adventurers many of them died. For some of them their dream was realized; others lost their heads in the pursuit.

One such man was Sir Walter Raleigh, the English soldier, seaman, courtier, author, and explorer who was the first to settle colonists in Virginia and to open Guiana to English enterprise. He was the brilliant favorite of Queen Elizabeth I.

Partly because of his work, men still dream of recapturing the wealth and treasure that lie waiting in a far-off land called Eldorado—the Land of Gold.

Let's take a look at his "diary" written after his exploration of Guiana, the area which today makes up Venezuela, Guyana and Dutch Surinam. These are his recollections, taken from *Discoverie of Guiana* (1596):

"The Empyre of Guiana is directly east from Peru towards the sea and lieth under the Equinoctial line, and it hath more abundance of Golde than any part of Peru, and as many or more great Cities than ever Peru had when it florished most; it is governed by the same lawes, and the Empereur and people observe the same religion, and the same forme and pollicies in government as was used in Peru, not differing in any part; and as I have beene assured by such of the Spanyardes as have seen Manoa, the emperiall Citie of Guinea, which the Spanyardes call el Dorado, that for the greatness, for the richness, and for the excellent seate, it farre exceedeth any of the world, at least of so much of the world as is knowen to the Spanish nation: it is founded upon a lake of salt water of 200 leagues long like unto mare caspiu. And if we compare it to that of Peru, and but reade the report of Francisco Lopez and others, it will seeme more than credible, and because we may judge of the one by the other, I thought good to insert part of the 120 chapter of Lopez in his generall historie of the Indies, wherein he describeth the court and magnificence of Guyanacapa, ancestor of the Empereur of Guiana. . . . All the vessels of his home, table, and kitchin were of gold and silver, and the meanest of silver and copper for strength and hardness of the mettal. He had in his wardroppe hollow statues of golde which seemed giants, and the figures in proportion and bignes of all the beastes, birdes, trees and hearbes, that the earth bringeth forth; and of all the fishes that the sea or waters of his kingdome breedeth. Hee had also ropes, budgets, chestes and troughs of golde, and sil-

ver, heapes of billets of golde that seemed woode, marked
out to burne.''

A most fantastic land indeed, and undoubtedly worth
conquering. The only problem, however, was its location;
for although Sir Walter was endowed with the gift of writing, he certainly was at a loss to pinpoint the land where
gold appeared to be a commonplace metal. Had he perhaps become a victim of his own imagination, or was
there really such a fabulous country somewhere beyond
the known boundaries of the South American jungle?

The gold fever that infected Pizarro's men when they
came face to face with the Inca treasures held them in its
grip until their death, for whenever their immediate desire
for possession of a certain treasure trove had been fulfilled, they were sure that there was always more to be
found beyond the next jungle or beyond the next city. In
the beginning the Indians innocently believed that the
Spaniards might possess a magic way to transform gold
into food, something that for them had *real* value. But
then they began to realize that, for some strange reason,
these white-skinned people wanted gold for gold's sake
alone—and they learned to take advantage of this fact.
Knowing that the mail-clad Spaniards were no match for
the steaming jungle, they teased them on, telling them
that there was much more gold to be had—a little more to
the north, or perhaps to the south; and if it wasn't there,
then it would be across the next mountain range . . . and
the Spaniards fell for it, time and time again. Inch by inch
they cut their way into the dense jungle, scaled steep
cliffs, and crossed seemingly impassable rivers, falling
prey to hostile Indians and treacherous snakes and jungle
fever . . . but the survivors always pushed onward
toward the next mountain range and the next steaming
jungle, leaving the bloating corpses of their compadres
behind to rot away in the choking foliage of the
unfriendly forest.

And while the conquistadores searched for the promised gold and their followers fell prey to the jungle in great numbers, the stories began to grow, as stories do when passed from one person to the next.

What had been a vague rumor of gold "somewhere behind the jungle" began to take on quite spectacular proportions when the sole survivor of one of the jungle expeditions stumbled back into camp with tales of having been rescued and cared for by the Incas in a secret City of Gold. Now even the skeptics began to believe. That the survivor had no proof for his story and had somehow not been able to bring back any of the gold presents his bene-factors had given him did not matter at all. He had found the City of Gold! It existed!

Suddenly the gold fever, which had slowly abated in the face of the continual failure of the many expeditions, began to rage again. Again eager adventurers left the rela-tive security of the cities and ventured out, this time cut-ting their way through the dense undergrowth of the jun-gle with only one aim: to find the lost City of Gold. But, as before, slow death, jungle fever, Indians and snakes took their toll, and the City of Gold remained a mystery.

It was not until 1535 that the first real break came. Sebastian de Belacazar, founder of Quito, capital of Ecuador, in a conversation with an Indian, heard of the king of a tribe in a far-distant region who sprinkled his body with gold dust once a year before going into a sacred mountain lake for a ceremonial cleansing. Reverently referring to the king as El Dorado—the Golden Man—the Indian was able to give only vague directions, but he did mention a mountain lake by the name of Guatavita.

A year later the search for the legendary Golden Man began in all earnest with an expeditionary force of nine hundred men led by Gonzalo Jiminez de Queseda; but by the time they finally reached a mountain lake which they judged to be Guatavita, malaria, swamp fever, snakes, and hostile natives had diminished the force to no more than two hundred men, most of whom were sick. Their discovery turned out to be a great disappointment, for aside from the deep blackness of the water, there was nothing about the lake or its vicinity to fit the description given by the Indian. The few deserted huts that stood on the water's edge hardly substantiated the romantic tales of torch-lit ceremonial processions to the accompaniment of clanging cymbals and native flutes in honor of the Golden King. There were no traces of the gold with which the king reportedly dusted himself before going into the sacred lake for a ceremonial cleansing to which he gave himself as a "sacrifice" for the sins of his people. If there had ever been any gold at all, it surely was not there now.

Again the search for El Dorado had hit a dead end. Could it be possible that not only the *City of Gold* but also the *Man of Gold* were nothing but the end result of a chain of rumors that had finally crystallized themselves into two specific targets? But rumors die hard, especially when they deal with the promise of immeasurable riches— and this rumor was now transmuted into a sketch and actually placed on a map! Without any solid foundation whatsoever, the cartographer Jodocus Hondius included a drawing of a lake of considerable size on his map entitled "New Map of the Country of Guiana Rich in Gold." He called the lake *Dorado* or *Laguna Parima* and placed an imperial city named Manoa on its shores. Now various other charts began to pinpoint Dorado and Manoa. Sure, the locations were not always the same, and sometimes the name was changed slightly—one of the maps referred to the lake as the Golden Sea—but they were there. Eventually, of course, the mapmakers were obliged to omit the imperial city of Manoa and Dorado Lake from their newer maps because their location could never be established with any degree of accuracy. Spanish soldiers had taken the rumors about the lake and Manoa to different areas of South America and had launched searches for the fabled places in both western and eastern parts of the continent, greatly complicating verification of the site.

Yet even though the lake supposedly discovered by de Queseda dimmed in the minds of the adventurers, the legend of the Golden King remained very much alive, thanks to the description of him given by Juan de Castellanos, a solder in the Spanish Indies who wrote of him in 1601:

"This is the king who went without garments in a boat upon a pool anointed all over with the essence of terebinthine over which a quantity of powdered gold had been cast in such a way as to cover him from head to foot and which made him shine like a sun . . . . In the evening he bathed in the waters of the lake where all the gold with which he had been covered dissolved away."

It was the romance and the challenge of finding the land of the king who "shone like the sun" that kept both the lake and El Dorado alive until they were finally fused into one location, *Eldorado, the Land of Gold.* By the beginning of the 1800s, small, poorly financed expeditions were forcing their way into the wilderness of South America in search of the renowned riches. But it was as if the fate of all seekers had been predestined, for these men died in their attempts, as had all those who had gone before them, and Eldorado remained as elusive as ever.

However, the fact that many of the Indians of South America were still using gold to forge their everyday eating utensils prompted small groups to form syndicates with the sole aim of draining Lake Guatavita. The idea was not so farfetched as it might seem. It had been tried in 1580 by Don Antonia Sepulveda, who, using Indian workers, cut a hole in the wall of the lake allowing much of the water to escape. At that time a number of gold objects and an egg-size emerald were reported to have been recovered from the lake bottom, but complications with the wall and problems with the Indian laborers forced the abandonment of the project. The more "modern" expeditions did not fare much better. One of them succeeded in draining sufficient water to expose a portion of the lake's bottom—but little else.

Disgusted, discouraged and broke, most of the interested parties retreated, giving their pride the time and distance to heal; and by the middle of the twentieth century, Eldorado had become little more than a myth. The King of Gold, the man who washed himself ceremoniously in the sacred water of Lake Guatavita, was accepted as nothing more than a figment of the imagination of an Indian who was overeager to please a gold-hungry Spaniard.

End of the story? No, not quite. Tradition tells us that whenever the Golden King went down into the sacred lake to wash off the gold with which he had been covered, the people would participate in the ceremony by throwing gold trinkets into the water as an additional sacrifice to the gods, and that this practice continued for at least 150 years. A quick calculation reveals that if 1,000 worshipers had each thrown at least three gold ornaments into the lake once a year for 150 years, the lake bottom must contain at least 450,000 gold objects. If Lake Guatavita's bottom shows nothing but mud—no gold—then perhaps the fabled lake has not yet been found, and a further exploration of the area as well as a further examination of the bottoms of other qualifying lakes with metal detectors might be called for.

Was there *really* a Golden King? Was there really a Man of Gold, as the Indian reported? It would have been a valid question before 1969, but in that year the cynics and unbelievers received a serious blow. Two farmers, exploring a cave near Bogota, Colombia, discovered a beautifully handcrafted model of a raft made entirely of gold. What really ties it in with the age-old search for El Dorado or Eldorado, however, are the golden figures on the craft. For positioned with their backs to an enthroned Golden King are eight oarsmen accompanying their sover-

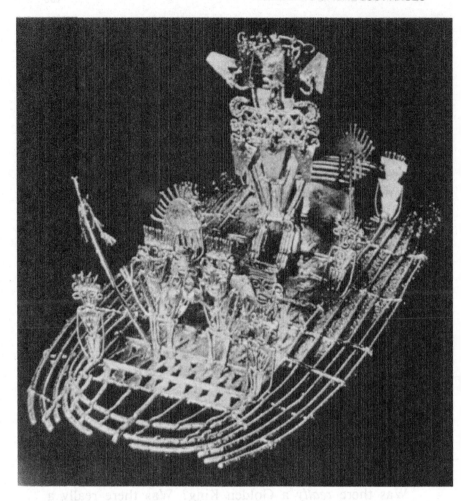

In 1969 two farm workers exploring a cave near Bogota, Colombia, discovered this small but solid gold model of the raft of El Dorado. The Man of Gold sits on his throne amidst the oarsmen, whose backs are all turned toward him. No doubt El Dorado was taken on a similar raft to the middle of the Sacred Lake.

eign on what may well be his annual ceremonial voyage to the middle of the lake, there to sacrifice his golden body to the gods!

Considering the price of gold, all planning for new expeditions with the aim of locating the real Sacred Lake and its thousands of gold artifacts is being done on a "need to know" basis, and is thus far limited to the boardrooms of banks and offices of South American financial tycoons.

With the finding of the golden raft, even the cynics are now beginning to show a more than casual interest in launching a truly scientific expedition using all the latest technology. "There are several lakes which may qualify to be *the* one, and we may end up checking every one of them with underwater metal-detection equipment," a spokesman for one interested group reported not so long ago. "To find the Land of Gold is out of the question, since that term came into being as a misinterpretation of El Dorado, the Man of Gold. But the lake is real; of that we have no doubt. The discovery of El Dorado's golden raft has convinced us."

Today's treasure hunters are not like the adventurous characters of the past. Now they're businessmen who look upon a possible treasure site as an investment or an expedition as a tax write-off—and for them the search for the sacred lake is indeed a worthwhile financial venture. If the tradition proves true and if our calculation of 450,000 is a realistic estimate of the number of gold objects that have been deposited in the lake, then the value of the lake treasure may well be in the neighborhood of $225 million. Perhaps the Land of Gold is there after all!

In Pursuit of Pharaoh's Army

The entire world is really a treasure hunter's paradise. I became strongly aware of this a number of years ago when I became involved in a strange yet fascinating search for an entire lost army.

It was after I had talked my way through Israeli customs and had grabbed my bags that I first noticed the wildly waving Ron Wyatt, standing tall amidst a crowd of bearded Hasidic Jews outside the terminal building at Ben Gurion Airport on the outskirts of Tel Aviv. Israel was old familiar territory—I had left many footprints there. In fact, I had gotten to know all of Palestine as if it were my own backyard during the many military and political newspaper assignments I had fulfilled there. Yet I had a different feeling about this trip. This was to be one without deadlines, without assassination plots, without definite time limits or curfews, and without the usual mad dashes to embassies, or to censorship or telegraph offices. This was going to be a trip simply to enjoy.

Ron, an amateur archaeologist and my fellow explorer in Israel, had visited my home on White Oak Mountain a few months earlier. "I have developed a new theory," he said, dropping his massive frame into the only chair in my office that could hold his weight—and survive. "I think I know the route the Israelites took through the Sinai desert after they left Egypt in or around 1425 B.C. and the spot where they finally crossed the Red Sea, pursued by the Egyptian army . . . ."

"But the Egyptians . . . " I began.

Ron interrupted me quickly.

"You mean they drowned? They surely did!" he admitted readily. "But that's exactly why I am so interested in that spot. *An entire army drowned there,* and since much of their gear as well as their war chariots were made of iron, bronze and gold, some of it must be on the bottom of the Red Sea where they crossed, and buried on the beaches on both sides. I want to go look for it. Want to join me and find the place?"

As a journalist with archaeology for a hobby, I could

think of nothing I'd rather do, and we soon arrived at a cohesive plan of action and decided on a target date. When the time finally arrived later on that year, Ron and his two sons and daughter flew ahead and I followed via a quick stop in western Europe to pick up some additional camera equipment.

Greeting Ron in the ovenlike heat of the Middle Eastern noonday sun, I handed him one of my bags and we ran across the parking lot and climbed into a rented van. It was not until later on that day in a hotel in Eilat that we had a chance to sit down quietly to compare notes and examine both our strategy and our theory. The scheme indeed had possibilities.

What we were interested in finding was evidence of one of the most pivotal events in ancient history, for if the Egyptians had been able to force the Hebrews back to Egypt, the history of the Middle East, and in fact the history of the civilized world, would have turned out quite differently.

The basic story of the Hebrews' escape from bondage in Egypt has been told time and time again; it has been the subject of many motion pictures, theatrical productions, and books, both fictional and factual. After 430 years of Egyptian captivity, the Hebrews, under Moses' leadership, finally rebelled and under the guidance of Jehovah asked the Pharaoh for permission to leave. The biblical book of Exodus, chapters 3 through 12, faithfully records their agonizing struggle for freedom, while Numbers 1:46 gives us the staggering number of people who followed Moses into the wilderness, away from the relative safety of Egypt, on the way to the Promised Land. In the nations of old—and even today in many countries in the Middle East—women were not included in any estimate of the number of people participating in a particular event or living in a specific area. The Hebrews were no different when they recorded the number of escapees, and the book of Numbers lists 603,550 men. Add to this the women and children, and a total of two million would not appear to be excessive.

But these people were all slaves, and when the word reached Pharaoh Amenhotep II that his Hebrew slaves had actually left the kingdom never to return, he vowed revenge. Comments the Jewish historian Flavius Josephus:

"But the Egyptians soon repented that the Hebrews were gone; and the king also was mightily concerned that this had been procured by the magic arts of Moses: so they resolved to go after them. Accordingly they took their weapons, and other warlike furniture, and pursued after them, in order to bring them back . . . and they thought they could easily overcome them, as they had no armour, and would be weary with their journey: so they made haste in their pursuit, and asked of everyone they met which way they were gone. And indeed that land was difficult to travel over, not only by armies by by single persons.

" . . . Now when the Egyptians had overtaken the Hebrews, they prepared to fight them, and by their multitude they drove them into a narrow place, for the number that pursued after them was SIX HUNDRED CHARIOTS, WITH FIFTY THOUSAND HORSEMEN, AND TWO HUNDRED THOUSAND FOOTMEN, ALL ARMED. They also seized on the passages by which they imagined the Hebrews might fly, shutting them up between inaccessible precipices and the sea: *for there was a ridge of mountains that terminated at the sea which were* impassable by reason of their roughness, and obstructed their flight. *Wherefore they pressed upon the Hebrews with their army, where the mountains were closed with the sea;* which army they placed at the chops of the mountains, so they might deprive them of any passage into the plain."

Seventeenth-century etching depicting the Red Sea closing in on the Pharaoh and his army during his pursuit of the Hebrews after their departure from Egypt.

After recalling Moses' prayer for help, Josephus continued,

" . . . he [Moses] smote the sea with his rod, which parted asunder at the stroke, and receiving those waters unto itself, left the ground dry, as a road and a place of flight for the Hebrews.

" . . . he went first of all into it, and bid the Hebrews to follow him along the divine road, and to rejoice at the danger their enemies that followed them were in."

And turning his attention to the Egyptian army, Josephus records:

" . . . the Egyptians supposed first that they were distracted, and were going rashly upon manifest destruction. But when they saw that they were going a great way without any harm, and that no obstacle or difficulty fell in their journey, they made haste to pursue them, hoping that the sea would be calm for them also. They put their horse foremost and went down themselves into the sea.

"Now the Hebrews, while these were putting on their armour, and therein spending their time, were before hand with them, and escaped them, and got first over to the land on the other side without any hurt.

" . . . but the Egyptians were not aware that they went into a road made for the Hebrews, and not for others . . . as soon, therefore, as ever the whole Egyptian army was within it, the sea flowed to its own place, and came down with a torrent raised by storms and wind, and encompassed the Egyptians. Showers of rain also came down from the sky, and dreadful thunders and lightning with flashes of fire. Thunderbolts were also darted upon them . . . . *And thus did all these men perish, so that there was not one man left to be a messenger of this calamity to the rest of the Egyptians.*"

It was the greatest single disaster that ever befell a nation, for in one blow the Pharaoh—the Egyptian king and commander-in-chief—and the priests who had accompanied the army and its entire elite fighting force had been totally destroyed without the enemy's having suffered a single casualty. *Roughly 251,000 men and more than 50,000 horses died that one night on a path through the Red Sea that was probably no wider than a few hundred yards and no more than twelve miles long!*

Looking back on the morning after the mass drowning, Josephus writes rather matter-of-factly:

"On the next day Moses gathered together the weapons of the Egyptians which were brought to the camp of the Hebrews by the current of the sea, and the force of the wind resisting it: so when he had ordered the Hebrews to arm themselves with them, he led them to Mount Sinai, in order to offer sacrifices to God.''

Historians are not in total agreement about the date of the Hebrews' exodus from Egypt, but it is generally accepted that it probably happened at the end of the reign of Pharaoh Amenhotep II, who ruled Egypt from 1450 to 1425 B.C. That the Egyptians did not mention this national tragedy in their records is no surprise, for the ancients seldom commemorated their defeats in stone inscriptions or painted hieroglyphics.

The theory on which Ron Wyatt was basing his exploratory trip into the Middle East was founded on two very obvious points made by Flavius Josephus and recorded in the Bible. Both mention that the Hebrew children went south from Egypt, through the desert, ending at the shore of the Red Sea in an area where *"the mountains were closed with the sea."* That the Red Sea at that time extended—in name at least—as far as Eilat at the top of the Gulf of Aqaba can be seen in I Kings 9:26, where it states that ''King Solomon made a navy of ships in Eziongeber, *which is beside Eloth, on the shore of the Red Sea,* in the land of Edom.''

Wyatt reasoned therefore that the Israelites had crossed the Sinai from west to east and had finally reached an area on the eastern coast (Gulf of Aqaba) where a mountain range met the sea. According to the record, the Egyptians had taken over the mountain peaks near the area to prevent the Hebrews from escaping. It also mentions that *after* they had crossed the Red Sea, Moses took them to *"Mt. Sinai in order to offer sacrifices to God."*

A careful examination of the eastern shore of the Sinai peninsula allows for only one place where two million people and their flocks can be gathered. It is the wide expanse of beach near Nuweba, the south end of which is closed off by steep mountains! Nearby is a wide and wild

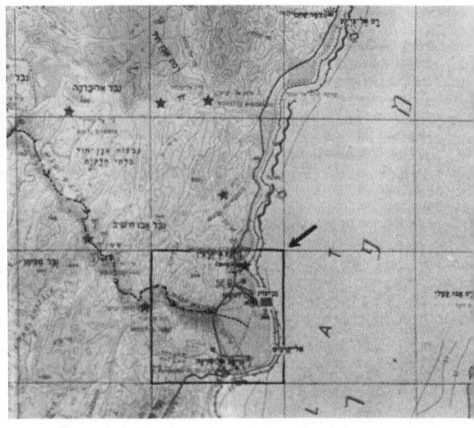

The area outlined in black *(note arrow)* is the only part of the western coast of the Sinai peninsula where two million people could have set up camp. It is interesting that the Red Sea is shallowest at this very point.

mountain gorge known as the Wadi Watir, an ancient dried-out riverbed that forms a natural roadway into the Sinai desert. What's more, the traditional Mt. Sinai is deep within the Sinai desert, while both the Bible and Josephus indicate that Moses took the Hebrews to Mt. Sinai *after* they crossed the Red Sea into what is now known as Saudi Arabia. Interestingly, not far from the opposite shore is a mountain known as Jebal El Lawz, a steep, forbidding peak. Is it perhaps possible that this is the Mt. Sinai that Moses speaks of?

There are many different theories regarding the possible location of the real Mt. Sinai, and Ron Wyatt's location wasn't all that farfetched. He held that the Israelites, after leaving Egypt, went down the western side of the Sinai along the Gulf of Suez and crossed the Sinai from west to east through its most rugged mountainous section by traveling over the dried-out riverbeds that run into each other. Their route, according to him, could well have gone via the Wadi Feiran, connecting with the Wadi El Akhdar, which in turn runs into the Wadi Salaqa, becomes the Wadi Zaranek, and eventually meets the Gulf of Aqaba via the well-known Wadi Watir. The Wadi Watir is the *only* wadi that ends at a wide beachlike expanse whose southernmost end is cut off by steep mountains. An

Beginning of the Wadi Watir, moving into the Sinai mountains from the beachlike expanse at the Dead Sea. At this point the wadi is smooth and can be traveled quite easily.

escaping horde of people arriving at the Red Sea via the Wadi Watir had only two choices: to be annihilated on the beach by the pursuing armies that could enclose it from the north, while it was hemmed in by mountains on the west and south; or to go forward into the water. There simply could have been no other.

Early the next morning we left Aqaba and headed south along the sandy coastline into the direction of Neviot, a camping and diving center, one of the choicest vacation spots for Israelis since the 1967 war, which had left the Sinai in Israeli hands. After checking into the availability of diving equipment, we moved on southward toward Nuweba, the most likely spot for the Red Sea crossing.

By now it was unbearably hot, and while the others made ready for the dive I took a good look at the surrounding area. There was no doubt that the expanse of beach between the Wadi Watir and Nuweba was big enough to accommodate two million overnight campers, together with their carts and animals. They might not have had an abundance of space in which to move around, but then I doubt that they would have wanted to move about very much anyway, for a three- or four-day trek through the rugged wadis isn't exactly like walking on a well-paved road. Also, their fear of the pursuing Egyptian army would have made them stick close together—and close to Moses, who had promised to lead them to safety.

Leaving the others to try out their equipment in the water, Ron and I moved on toward the mountains that cut off the beach on its southern end. Though not totally blocked, the narrow strip of rocky sand that remained at the foot of the mountains would not have been wide enough to support the flight of two million slaves trying to escape an avenging army. The rocks bore a striking resemblance to the ones described by Josephus as having halted any further movement of the Hebrew people.

I remember wondering, as I looked at the vast body of water, whether it might have been just as quiet when Moses struck the water with his staff. From our vantage point, the hazy mountains of the coast of Saudi Arabia could easily be seen ten or twelve miles across the rippling sea. Could this really be the place where 251,000 Egyptians had met their doom 3,400 years ago? Was this the area where an angry Pharaoh and his priests led one of the best equipped armies of their time into a battle from which there was no return? Not even for a courier?

Two hours later I stood quietly at the water's edge while Ron and his son Danny adjusted their oxygen tanks for their first dives into the Red Sea. It was early afternoon, and the wind had retired behind the Sinai mountains. The only ripples to disturb the surface of the water were the ever-widening circles that betrayed the spots where the divers had disappeared, and a trail of rising air bubbles traced their slow progress along the rocky bottom.

Ron was the first to break the surface. He grabbed the ropes that hung down from the yellow rubber boat I had rowed to the area of investigation—about two hundred feet from the beach. "It's quite clean on the bottom," he breathed excitedly, after taking off his mask and securing himself with the ropes. *"We've moved slowly, and the uneven bottom shows a great number of uneven shapes that have completely been covered with coral. There's one that has the round shape of a wagon wheel with a hub in the middle—all crusted over—and right close to it is a big half-circular piece of something that could well be the front armor section of a chariot."* He reached into the boat for his underwater camera gear and went back down.

In the boat, we followed Ron's bursting bubbles, first moving in the direction of the rocks, then ever so slowly toward the beach. When I pulled the raft ashore and Ron had emerged from the water, we discussed what he had seen. "There was a greenish mess moving in while I was still down there," Ron explained as he peeled off his wet suit. "Probably algae of some sort. Anyway, by the time I got the camera and went back down, it was as if I were swimming in the middle of a greenish layer of soup. Nothing was distinguishable—I couldn't even get a good reading on the light meter . . . "

The next day we hired a glass-bottomed boat at the Neviot diving center and motored out toward the target area. The sea was quite choppy; and despite the blazing sun, the ocean breeze chilled us to the bone. Our eyes and our concentration were constantly focused on the two-by-five-foot section of plexiglass in the bottom of the boat that was supposed to give us a clear view of the Red Sea's rugged bottom; but long before we reached our target area, greenish murk moved in, hindering our view. After we had thrown out the anchor on the previous day's site, the divers went down once more, this time with cameras at the ready. But conditions were even worse than they had been the day before. The algae seemed to extend for miles. It was obvious that it would be days before the water would be sufficiently clear to search the bottom again.

Back at the diving center we reevaluated our strategy. In order not to lose valuable time, we decided to check out the wadi connection between western and eastern Sinai; and after the usual haggling, we entrusted our lives to the hands of Allah and his servant Ibrahim, a dirty-white-robed Bedouin. Ibrahim owned an old jeep with a coughing engine but a set of reasonably good tires that just might make it. A mixture of Arabic, English, gestures, greenbacks, and a map of the Sinai produced not only smiles but also a general agreement as to the route we would take in our effort to duplicate at least a part of the trajectory of the Hebrew people—only this time in reverse.

When we left the main road the next morning and moved into the Wadi Watir, it was like entering a moon landscape. The middle and southern part of the Sinai are rugged beyond compare; the reddish-gray peaks that characterize the area appear harsh, cruel, and uninhabitable. They are of bewildering height, towering with awesome grandeur above a lone traveler attempting to find his way through the mountains.

With great skill—undoubtedly the result of much practice on this type of terrain—Ibrahim guided the bouncing jeep across the rock-lined riverbed of the wadi on the way to the Wadi Zeranek. Our eyes kept moving from one rock to another as we worried about possible avalanches or rockslides. As soon as we turned the first bend in the wadi, we began to feel utterly lost. Every mountain looked exactly like the one we had just passed, and an indefinably uneasy feeling came over us as we penetrated deeper and deeper into the wilderness. Only occasionally was the monotony of the ride interrupted—by the sight of a lone ibex silhouetted against a high cliff, or a vulture circling overhead, waiting patiently; or by the nervous coughing of the jeep's engine.

And so we continued, hour after hour, until suddenly Ibrahim decided to stop. He had shouted a few hasty words at a couple of Bedouin shepherds we'd passed a few minutes back, and as soon as we turned the next bend he pulled the key out of the dashboard, threw up his hands, and started a tirade in Arabic which, even though we didn't understand all the words, indicated clearly enough that he'd had it and wanted to go back to Neviot. We still had enough gas to get to the next Israeli-manned oasis and more than sufficient water and could therefore see no reason to cancel our plans at this point.

But Ibrahim had a different idea. From his viewpoint, he was in friendly territory. This was the area of his tribe. He was *home,* and we didn't count; we were simply strangers with wallets full of cash and expensive camera gear and camping equipment. Our entry into the Sinai had not been recorded by anyone. No one could prove that we had ever been there. Only the Bedouins at the diving center knew, and they were his friends and wouldn't talk.

For the better part of an hour we argued in a variety of languages and gestures, but nothing worked. The ignition key remained tightly clutched in his hands as he kept reiterating that he was going back to Neviot! It was then that I began to notice his eyes darting back and forth to the mountainside where the Arab goatherds had appeared earlier. Now I also noticed the long shiny knife that had been carefully hidden in the folds of his white robe. Were we being set up for something? There certainly were enough rocks to conceal two bodies, and among the three of them we could quickly be disposed of.

Ron and I acted at the same time. Before Ibrahim could react, Ron had jumped into the jeep and reached for the lug wrench, while I grabbed the gasoline can and a book of matches, and we both turned on Ibrahim. Ron held the wrench over his head while I uncorked the gas.

"We'll go back to Neviot," Ron shouted at the frightened Arab, "but you will take us!" and dragging the shaking Arab to the front seat, he forced him to start the aging vehicle and turn it around. Ibrahim never had a chance to use his knife or call for help, for with the lug wrench held but inches over his head and the opened can of gasoline and the matches right next to him, he really didn't have much choice. Suddenly trouble was looking in his direction, and in the face of our insistent prodding and constant threats he moved on.

But the closer we got to the beginning of the Wadi Watir, the more resistant he became. He very obviously did not want to leave his tribal territory. We were just making the last gradual bend in the wadi when we heard the muted roar of a distant engine. When the curve straightened, there, perhaps five hundred yards from us, was a roving Israeli armored truck, a half-track, filled with heavily armed soldiers. Hurriedly I stood up and waved at them, signaling them to stop and wait. For a moment it seemed as if Ibrahim might make a run for it, but the weight of the lug wrench on his skull changed his mind. I grabbed the wheel and turned the jeep in the direction of the patrol.

A minute later we came to a halt in front of the truck, and the soldiers surrounded our jeep, guns at the ready. It is at moments like these that I am most grateful for my military press credentials: they have the ability to create instant understanding. Ibrahim's protests were vastly outweighed by our anger and the armed might of the Israelis. The lietenant in charge spoke Hebrew, English and Arabic and had no trouble understanding what Ibrahim had had in mind for us. "You shouldn't have gone into the Sinai without being armed," he cautioned. "Next time come by and see us and we'll give you an M-16 to take along. Too many unarmed civilians have disappeared in the Sinai. After all, it is still enemy territory!"

Forced to refund the money we had paid him for our trip through the Sinai, Ibrahim spat a stream of curses in our direction. Even Mohammed would have been ashamed of this son of Ishmael.

Even though our trip had been cut short, we were convinced from what we had seen of the interior of the Sinai that travel by foot through the wadis is in fact possible. The wadi route certainly has merit when considering the escape route of the children of Israel. We also made two more dives into the Red Sea—but each time the green algae created a zero-visibility situation. Our diving season had come to an end.

Today (May 1982) the Sinai has changed hands again and is no longer Israeli territory. The Neviot diving center

Ron Wyatt disappearing into a narrow segment of the tunnel he
is excavating near Old Jerusalem.

is now Egyptian, and all the cards are back in the hands
of Ibrahim. Perhaps someone else ought to make the next
dive . . .

Ron Wyatt phoned me again recently. "Rene, I've got
another project in mind. Again in the Middle East. Can I
interest you in joining me?" Foolish question!

A day later we were sitting again in the quiet of my
office discussing his latest treasure-hunting plans. Without knowing anything at all about the finding of the copper scrolls or their treasure locations, he had started his
own snooping around Old Jerusalem, hoping to find
some of the temple treasure that was buried prior to the
Babylonian and Roman raids on Jerusalem.

"I've been digging in Jerusalem for two seasons now—crawling underground like a mole—and have opened up an old cave that keeps branching out into smaller caves and a large room," he explained excitedly. "It is located not too far from the old Damascus Gate, and the site has been used by the owner as a garbage dump for many years. I've had a strange feeling about it ever since I saw it for the first time, for it's an ideal hiding place. So I looked up the owners and asked if I could have their permission to clean it out and do some digging in the cave. They readily agreed, and my two excavation seasons are now beginning to produce results."

Both Ron and I had been to the site several times in the past, and when he described it to me I was aghast. I had passed that very place just about every time I had been to Jerusalem, as do 200,000 other Christians every year when they visit the nearby Christian shrine; but the idea of actually digging there had never occurred to me.

Ron opened an envelope and placed a collection of photographs on the table. All were shots taken inside a narrow cave barely big enough for Wyatt's heavy frame. "I brought these with me to give you an idea what the cave is all about," he explained, "but I want you to look especially at this one!" The photograph he had singled out revealed a large cavelike area halfway filled with rocks. Since the camera had been tied to the end of a stick and shoved through a narrow opening in the cave, the photo was out of focus. The hard light of the electronic flash, however, had illuminated not only the roughly hewn ceiling and walls but also part of a large rectangular gold object that was still partially hidden by the rocks that covered the floor. Its reflection was brilliant yellow against the reddish-brown of the rock. Because copper and bronze do not survive the ages without turning green or brown, the bright yellow shine that reflected the light was undoubtedly indicative of a golden object.

"I have taken sensitive metal detectors into the cave," said Ron, "and I got soundings from different places. I have also probed into the mass of loose rock in one of the rooms, and there seems to be a chest underneath the rocks, about three by six feet in size. It will take quite a while to clear it out, but it will be worth it."

Wyatt's permission to excavate the cave is good for only one more season; after that, the cave has to be filled in again and will probably regain its former "prominence" as a garbage dump.

And the treasure—if it can be extracted from the cave? "I am not really after the money," commented Ron after we discussed mutual plans for the final phase of the operation. "I think I have stumbled on some of the lost temple treasure; and if that is true, then it may well be a major find of historical value. To me that's more important than just the financial rewards."

EPILOGUE

By the time this book goes to press, the final phase of Wyatt's salvage operation should be in full swing.

However, this dig is only one of many that can be conducted by dedicated amateurs. With the technological advances that have come as part of the scientific development of the twentieth century, a whole array of new tools has become available to anyone with the determination to discover the riches of the past.

Whole civilizations have come and gone. Entirely new cultures have replaced others of equal greatness and importance, but in many cases Mother Earth has conveniently opened up her faults and crevasses and quietly conspired with history to cover up her tracks.

But whereas in former years we as amateurs could only *dream* of finding the treasures of the past, we now have the ability and the opportunity to participate in the search. No longer is the digging confined to the professionals, who—in their dusty museum libraries—dream up their plans for a new excavation and then follow up by taking their theoretical approach to the field and using methods which often limit the results. Few archaeological field teams take full advantage of space-age discovery tools. This of course gives the unconventional, inventive and technically minded amateur a decided advantage. The latter is also free of the stringent rules and regulations that govern the archaeological profession. Taking their four-wheel-drive vehicles into the hinterlands or hard-to-reach places, using metal detectors, current-resistivity meters and the old-fashioned unscientific "hunch"—a tool seldom recognized as such by the professionals—amateurs are now beginning to get results that put the professionals to shame.

The world is beginning literally to open up, and the results will help illuminate our dim understanding of history. A careful look at the finely handcrafted art left us by the Egyptians, Greeks, Scythians, Celts, Incas and others should be proof enough that our forefathers were members of cultures that were often far advanced. By having lost our historical links to our early ancestors, we have lost much of our heritage; and in excavating for the past, we may begin to find ourselves.

What we will eventually do *with* and *to* the human race—once all the pieces of the puzzle are in and the new composite picture of humanity's sojourn on Planet Earth has been put together—is a question only time can answer. Our historical performance thus far hasn't been so praiseworthy as to give us much confidence.

Perhaps the overall view of the greatness of our past as seen through the treasures of the ancients will inspire us to greater heights; on the other hand, perhaps nothing can prevent our extinction, and we will follow our nearly forgotten ancestors to our doom. Here the future, not history, will have the last word.

BIBLIOGRAPHY

Allegro, John Marco. *The Treasure of the Copper Scroll.* New York: Doubleday & Company, 1960.

_____. *The Dead Sea Scrolls.* London: Pelican Books, 1956.

"America's Prehistoric Pilgrims," *Science Digest,* May 1981.

"Ancient Bulgaria's Gold Treasures," *National Geographic Magazine,* July 1980.

"Ark of Covenant Found in Palestine Not Original One." *Chattanooga Free Press* (UPI), August 2, 1981.

"Asteroid Gold Rush." *Science Digest,* December 1981.

Bacon, Edward. *Digging for History: Archaeological Discoveries Throughout the World, 1945-1959.* New York: John Day, 1960.

Baudin, Louis. *Socialist Empire: Incas of Peru.* New York: Van Nostrand Reinhold Co., 1961.

Belzoni, G. *Narrative of the Operations and Recent Discoveries within the Pyramids, Temples, Tombs, and Excavations in Egypt and Nubia; and of a Journey to the Coast of the Red Sea, in Search of the Ancient Berenice; and Another to the Oasis of Jupiter Ammon.* 2 Vols. London: John Murrey, 1821.

Blaser, Lawrence W. *The Mystery of the Ark of the Covenant.* Englewood, Colorado: Ark Enterprises, 1978.

Budge, Sir E. A. Wallis. *The Queen of Sheba and Her Only Son Menyelek* (Kebra Nagast), translation. London: Philip Lee Warner, 1932.

Carter, George. *Egyptian Gold Seekers in the Pacific.* Occasional Publication of the Epigraphic Society, Vol. 2, No. 27.

Carter, Mary Ellen. *Edgar Cayce on Prophecy.* New York: Paperback Library, 1968.

Ceram, C. W. *Gods, Graves and Scholars.* New York: Alfred A. Knopf, 1968.

China Reconstructs, Vol. XXXI, No. 2, February 1982.

Cordan, Wolfgang. *Der Nil,* Dusseldorf: Eugen Diederichs Verlag, 1956.

Dechelette, Joseph. *Manuel d'archaeologie prehistorique Cletique at Gallo-Romaine.* Paris: Picard, 1913.

Dillon, Myles, and Nora Chadwick. *The Celtic Realms.* New York: New American Library, 1967.

Doberer, K. K. *The Goldmakers.* London: Nicholson & Watson, 1948.

Encyclopedia Britannica: Chicago: Encyclopedia Britannica, Inc., 1969.

"Everyday Life in Bible Times," Washington, D.C.: National Geographic Society, 1967.

"Evidence Proves It: Columbus Was a Latecomer." *Family Weekly,* January 29, 1978.

Fell, Barry. *America B.C.* New York: Pocket Books, 1976.

———. *Saga America.* New York: Times Books, 1980.

"From These Hills." *Biblical Archaeology Review,* June 1978.

Funk & Wagnalls New Encyclopedia. New York: Funk & Wagnalls, Inc., 1971.

Giles, L. A. *Gallery of Chinese Immortals.* London: John Murrey, 1948.

"Gold, Brazil's Big Find." *Parade,* March 29, 1981.

"Gold in the Athena Parthenos," *American Journal of Archaeology,* 1977.

Greece and Rome. Washington, D.C.: National Geographic Society, 1967.

Harrison, W. "Detection of Graves and Underground Objects by Dowsing." *New Horizons* (Journal of the New Horizons Research Foundations incorporating transactions of the Toronto Society for Physical Research), Vol. 1, No. 4 (July 1974), pp. 155-159.

"Has the U.S. Geological Survey Found King Solomon's Gold Mines?" *Biblical Archaeology Review,* Vol. III, No. 3, September 1977.

"Hoard of Gold Coins of Philip and Alexander from Corinth, A," *American Journal of Archaeology,* 1974.

Holy Bible, Revised Standard Version, with Old Testament Apocrypha.

Josephus, Flavius. *Jewish History,* Amsterdam, 1720.

Keller, Werner. *The Bible as History,* New York: Bantam, 1964.

Kondratov, A. M. *Lost Civilizations* (Rus.), Moscow, 1968.

"Legendary Vein of Gold Said 'Found,' " *Chattanooga Free Press,* March 17, 1981.

Logan, Daniel. *The Reluctant Prophet.* New York: Avon, 1968.

McIntyre, Loren. *The Incredible Incas and Their Timeless Land.* Washington, D.C.: The National Geographic Society, 1975.

Milik, J. T. *Ten Years of Discovery in the Wilderness of Judea.* London: SCM Press, 1959.

_____"The Copper Scrolls." Revue Biblique, 1959.

Noorbergen, Rene. *Secrets of the Lost Races.* New York: Bobbs-Merrill, 1978.

_____. *You Are Psychic.* New York: William Morrow & Company, 1973.

Ostrander, Sheila, and Lynn Schroeder. *Psychic Discoveries Behind the Iron Curtain.* Englewood Cliffs, N.J.: Prentice-Hall, 1970.

"Periscope on the Etruscan Past." *National Geographic Magazine,* September 1959.

Pluzhnikov, Aleksandr Ivanovich. "Possibilities for and Results of the Use of the Biophysical Method in Researching and Restoring Historical and Architectural Monuments." *The American Dowser,* 1974.

Proceedings of the Parapsychological Institute of the State University of Utrecht. The Netherlands: No. 1, December 1960.

"Psychic Archaeology," *Psychic Magazine,* September/October 1975.

Raleigh, Walter. *The Historie of the World,* in 5 books. London: Walter Burre, 1614.

"Regal Treasures from a Macedonian Tomb," *National Geographic Magazine,* July 1978.

Rhine, Joseph Banks. *New World of the Mind.* London: William Sloane, 1953.

Robinson, Lytle. *Edgar Cayce Story of the Origin and Destiny of Man.* New York: Coward, McCann & Geoghegan, Inc., 1972.

Rothenberg, Beno. *God's Wilderness.* New York: Thomas Nelson & Sons, 1962.

Sarianidi, V. I. *Raskopi Tilla tepe v Severnom Afganistane.* Moscow: Institute of Archaeology, USSR Academy of Sciences, 1972.

Schwartz, Stephen A. *The Secret Vaults of Time.* New York: Grosset & Dunlap, 1978.

S.D.A. Bible Commentary. Washington, D.C.: Review & Herald Publishing Assoc., 1953.

"Search of Solomon's Lost Treasures," *Biblical Archaeology Review,* July/August 1980.

"Sharp Eyes Find Ancient Treasure on the Beach," *Biblical Archaeological Review.*

"Slice of Culture 3,000 Years Thick," *National Geographic Magazine,* July 1980.

Stearn, Jess. *Edgar Cayce: The Sleeping Prophet.* New York: Bantam Books, 1968.

The World's Last Mysteries. New York: Reader's Digest, 1978.

Tomas, Andrew. *We Are Not the First.* New York: Bantam, 1973.

Vermes, G. *The Dead Sea Scrolls in English.* Harmondsworth, England: Penguin Books, 1962.

Von Daniken, Erich. *Chariots of the Gods.* New York: Bantam, 1970.

_____. *The Gold of the Gods.* New York: Bantam, 1974.

_____. *Signs of the Gods.* New York: G. P. Putnam's Sons, 1980.

Von Hagen, V. W. *Highway of the Sun.* New York: Duell, Sloan & Pierce, 1955.

_____. *Realm of the Incas.* New York: Mentor, 1957.

Werner, E. T. C. *Myths and Legends of China.* London: George G. Harrap, 1922.

White, Ellen G. *Patriarchs and Prophets.* Washington, D.C.: Review & Herald Publishing Assoc.

World Book Encyclopedia. Chicago, Ill.: Field Enterprises Ed. Corp., 1971.

INDEX

We'd love to have you download our catalog of titles we publish at:

www.TEACHServices.com

or write or email us your thoughts, reactions, or criticism about this or any other book we publish at:

TEACH Services, Inc.
254 Donovan Road
Brushton, NY 12916

info@TEACHServices.com

or you may call us at:

518/358-3494

Produced in partnership with
LNFBooks.com

CPSIA information can be obtained
at www.ICGtesting.com
Printed in the USA
BVOW09s0222261117
501262BV00013B/436/P